SHORTCUTS TO SU(

To Kill a Mockingbird
Exam Guide
For Junior Certificate

Allyson Prizeman

GILL EDUCATION

Gill Education
Hume Avenue
Park West
Dublin 12

Gill Education is an imprint of M.H.Gill & Co.

www.gilleducation.ie

© Allyson Prizeman 2009

978 07171 4587 4

Print origination by Carrigyboy Typesetting Services

The paper used in this book is made from the wood pulp of managed forests. For every tree felled, at least one tree is planted, thereby renewing natural resources.

Contents

1. Historical Background

The Economy

The novel *To Kill a Mockingbird* is set in the southern American state of Alabama in the 1930s, during the Great Depression. The economy was in ruins following the Wall Street Crash of 1929 when the stock markets crashed. The Depression was a time of widespread poverty and unemployment across the United States, and many people lost their land, their homes and their jobs.

Racism

In addition to these problems, America was also a deeply racist, prejudiced society. Slavery had been abolished following the Civil War in 1865, but African-Americans had not achieved equal rights in the United States, especially in the southern states like Alabama. For instance, segregation was still practised in southern states; black and white people attended separate schools and churches, the army was segregated and black people were not allowed to vote or be members of a jury. They had no say in how society was run.

Most white people regarded blacks as inferior in every way, and while black people were no longer slaves, they continued to work as servants in white people's homes and did not enjoy the same rights or liberties as white people.

The Civil Rights Movement

The novel is set in the 1930s, but it was actually written in the late 1950s, during the Civil Rights Movement. The Civil Rights Movement, led by preacher and activist, Martin Luther King, was a peaceful movement in which African-Americans organised themselves and demonstrated against racial inequality and segregation. It was triggered, in part, by a black woman called Rosa Parks who lived in Montgomery, Alabama. In 1955, Rosa Parks was arrested and placed in jail because she decided to sit in the white section of a bus and refused to move when the driver told her to. African-Americans in Montgomery organised themselves to protest against her arrest and decided to boycott all city buses. Boycotting was a non-violent but effective means of protest and it united black citizens in the fight against racial inequality. In 1956, the Supreme Court outlawed segregation on local bus lines.

After the success of the Montgomery boycott, the struggle for racial equality continued into the 1960s. Harper Lee supported the Civil Rights Movement, and her book exposed the ugly reality of racism, ignorance and injustice in the southern states at that time. (In the novel, Atticus warned his children that some day white people would have to pay the price for their treatment of black people.) In 1964, the Civil Rights Act made racial discrimination illegal, and in 1965 black people in the South were given the right to vote.

Life in the Southern States

While Maycomb was not a real town, it was typical of southern American towns such as Monroeville, where Harper Lee grew up. These towns were predominantly Christian and conservative. Most of their white inhabitants did not welcome change. Their wealth had been built on the labour of black slaves and they wanted black people to stay in their place and accept the master-slave relationship. It suited white people to regard African-Americans as inferior beings who were only fit to serve white families and work in the fields. The Civil Rights Movement challenged this kind of thinking and the inequality and injustice that resulted from it. For generations, black people had turned to Christianity for comfort, believing that a better world awaited them in the next life. Civil Rights activists encouraged black people to demand justice in their own lifetime, on earth.

2. Plot Summary

Part One

The novel opens in the mid-1930s when Scout is six and Jem is ten. The children live in Maycomb, Alabama, with their father Atticus, a lawyer. They are minded by their black maid, Calpurnia, because their mother is dead. The children enjoy an innocent, carefree childhood with their friend, Dill, who spends his summers in Maycomb. Their only concern is to make Boo Radley, the neighbourhood recluse, leave his house.

Scout starts school but she hates it. Over time, the children find mysterious gifts in a tree outside the Radley house. The following summer, Dill returns and the children use their imagination to re-enact scenes from Boo's life. On Dill's last night, the children sneak into Boo's garden, and Jem loses his trousers. Jem is shot at by Boo's older brother, Mr Nathan Radley, as he tries to escape. The gifts continue to appear in the tree until the children leave a 'thank you' note there for Boo. After this, Mr Nathan Radley fills the hole with cement.

During the winter, it snows for the first time since 1885 and Miss Maudie's house goes on fire. While the children stand in the snow, watching her house, they don't notice Boo Radley placing a blanket on Scout's shoulders.

At school, Scout fights other children for calling her father a 'nigger-lover'. She learns that Atticus is defending a black man, Tom Robinson, who is accused of raping a white girl, Mayella Ewell. She doesn't understand the details, but Atticus explains that this case is very important to him.

In February, Atticus saves the town from a 'mad dog' that has rabies. For the first time, the children see their father as a hero. Jem vandalises Mrs Dubose's garden and is punished for it. When she dies, the children learn that she was a brave woman who had conquered drug addiction.

Part Two

The children visit Calpurnia's church. Aunt Alexandra comes to stay. Tension is mounting in the run-up to the trial and the children get used to people pointing fingers at them. Dill runs away from home and is allowed to stay with Scout and Jem for a while. The night before the trial, a group of men from Old Sarum try to intimidate Atticus but they change their minds when Scout gets involved.

People from the whole county come to see the trial. Mayella insists that Tom raped her and beat her up, and Mr Ewell claims that he saw Tom doing this. There is no medical evidence that this happened and Mayella's story is vague and inconsistent. It becomes clear that Mayella was brutally beaten on the right side of her face. Mr Ewell is left-handed and Tom cannot use his left hand because of a disability. Despite the lack of evidence, the all-white jury convicts Tom of rape, a capital offence in Alabama.

After the trial, Tom is sent to prison and awaits his appeal. Bob Ewell threatens to get revenge on Atticus. He also harrasses Tom's wife, Helen, and he is suspected of watching Judge Taylor's house. One day, Tom is shot while trying to run away from prison. There is no sympathy for him among the people of Maycomb.

On the way home from a Hallowe'en pageant, the children are followed and attacked by Bob Ewell. He tries to stab Scout through her wire costume. Boo, who has also followed them, attacks Bob, saving the children's lives. Jem is knocked unconscious and breaks his arm. Bob Ewell is found dead, stabbed by his own knife. Scout finally meets Boo while Jem is sleeping. The Sheriff convinces Atticus that Bob fell on his own knife and they agree to tell no one about Boo's part in Ewell's death. Boo's privacy is respected and he is allowed to return to his normal life as a recluse. Scout falls asleep, aware that most people are good when you get to know them.

3. Summary and Analysis of Chapters

The novel is divided into Parts One and Two. Part One spans Chapters One to Eleven and it concentrates on the childhood experiences of Jem and Scout, their obsession with Boo Radley, the people of Maycomb and their attitudes and way of life. We are introduced to central characters like Atticus, Calpurnia, Miss Maudie and Dill. Part One portrays a time of innocence as well as a time of learning and growth for the children. The children are slowly learning not to judge someone until you have walked in their shoes for a while.

Part One

Chapter One

The novel starts with a first-person narration by Scout, whose real name is Jean Louise Finch. The story will be told from Scout's point of view as she looks back on 'the summer Dill came' and the events leading up to Jem's broken arm. The setting of the novel is Maycomb, Alabama (a southern state of the USA) during the 1930s.

Scout and her family

The opening chapter introduces us to Scout's family background, her life with Jem, Atticus and Calpurnia and the world of Maycomb. We learn a number of important details about Scout's life: her mother died when she was two and she lives with her father, Atticus, and her brother, Jem. The children are minded by their black maid, Calpurnia. At the start of the novel, Scout is almost six and Jem is nearly ten. Atticus is a lawyer and his family has lived in Maycomb for several generations. In Chapter One, Scout tells us about Atticus's ancestor Simon Finch, who came to Maycomb to establish his homestead, Finch's Landing. Scout tells us that Simon started out with three slaves, a reminder that slavery had been part and parcel of southern life and would form the basis for race relations in the South. She also points out the contradiction, overlooked by Simon, of a Christian man trading in human beings.

In this chapter, we learn that Scout and Calpurnia don't get along: 'Our battles were epic and one-sided. Calpurnia always won, mainly because Atticus always took her side.'

Scout and Jem make a new friend in Dill, who would spend every summer in Maycomb, staying with his Aunt Rachel.

Maycomb

Maycomb is a fictional town, but it is closely based on Monroeville, the small southern town where Harper Lee grew up. Life in Maycomb is described as dull and uneventful. People are nosey and like to gossip. White people have a relaxed way of life, but there is not a lot of money – this is the Great Depression of the 1930s.

Boo Radley

This chapter introduces us to the mysterious Radley family, and to the children's fascination with Boo. The Radley house is dark and neglected and local rumours suggest that 'a malevolent phantom' lives inside. Children are terrified of this house and will never climb over the fence to steal pecan nuts or retrieve a ball. The Radleys 'kept to themselves' and this is unheard of in Maycomb. Mr Radley would leave the house at 11.30 every morning for groceries, but Mrs Radley never came out, and Arthur Radley, or 'Boo', has not been seen for years.

Boo's background is explained. When he was a teenager, he got involved in a gang. His gang got up to mischief, carried out pranks and drank whiskey; they were not very threatening or dangerous but they shocked the people of Maycomb, who weren't used to this sort of behaviour. One night, Boo and his friends were arrested for crashing a car, and the town decided that 'something had to be done'. The reaction of the community was typical of a conservative, narrow-minded town. The boys were sent to an industrial school as punishment, but Mr Radley did not want the family name to be disgraced, so he promised the judge that he would keep his son out of trouble. Boo was 'not seen again for fifteen years'.

While it is not directly stated in this chapter, it is clear that Boo spent his adult life being punished for having disgraced the family in his youth. Mr Radley must have been a cruel, harsh father, because when he dies Calpurnia says, 'There goes the meanest man ever God blew breath into'. After his death, he is replaced by his son, Mr Nathan Radley, who is said to be the exact same as his father.

Despite the children's fear of Boo and the Radley place, Dill is determined to 'make him come out'. He wants to see what he looks like. Dill dares Jem to touch the house and Jem can't refuse a dare because he does not want to look like a coward. He runs into the garden, touches the house and runs back out. As the children look back at the house, they see a tiny, almost invisible flick of a window shutter. Their Boo Radley adventure has begun . . .

KEY QUOTATIONS

'Atticus was related by blood or marriage to nearly every family in the town.'

'Maycomb was an old town, but it was a tired old town when I first knew it . . . People moved slowly then . . . There was no hurry, for there was nowhere to go, nothing to buy and no money to buy it with.'

'Dill gave us the idea of making Boo Radley come out.'

'Inside the house lived a malevolent phantom. People said he existed but Jem and I had never seen him.'

'Radley pecans would kill you. A baseball hit into the Radley yard was a lost ball and no questions asked.'

Chapter Two

Scout starts school with eager anticipation – 'I never looked forward more to anything in my life' – but she is bitterly disappointed by the experience. Her new teacher, Miss Caroline Fisher, is not impressed that Scout can already read, and warns Scout that her father must stop 'teaching' her how to read. Scout is devastated, as she loves reading and cannot remember a time when she could not read. She can also write, but this is a disadvantage too, as the class is going to spend the year learning to 'print' letters. She will not be allowed to write all year in school.

In this chapter, we learn about the effects of poverty on children like Walter Cunningham. Walter has no shoes, he has 'hookworms' from walking around barefoot and he comes to school every day without lunch because his family cannot afford it. When Miss Fisher tries to lend Walter money for lunch, Scout gets into even more trouble for speaking out and explaining that Walter is a Cunningham, and the Cunninghams will not borrow anything that they cannot pay back. Of course, Miss Caroline does not understand this: she is an outsider from North Alabama and knows nothing about Maycomb and its people.

We see that Maycomb people are very suspicious of outsiders. Miss Fisher is actually from the same state as the children, but she might as well be from another planet. The children have inherited Maycomb's attitudes, and learnt to suspect people from North Alabama because of their history. This tells us two things about Maycomb: it is a very insular, close-knit town where everyone knows everyone else's business, and its people's prejudice is rooted in the past. As the novel progresses, the importance of one's history and background to Maycomb people will come up again.

KEY QUOTATIONS

'The Cunninghams are country folks, farmers, and the crash hit them hardest.' (Atticus)

Chapter Three
Scout beats Walter up in the school yard, because she feels it's his fault she got into trouble with Miss Caroline. When Jem intervenes to stop her, we see that Jem's role as Scout's older brother is to influence her and show maturity. Scout is shocked when Jem then invites Walter home for dinner.

As Walter dines with the Finches, we learn more about life for the 'country folks' during the Depression. Walter can never pass first grade because he has to miss school every spring to help on the farm. Atticus speaks to him as though he is an adult; this is because children like Walter work hard and have adult responsibilities. Walter pours syrup all over his dinner, and this shows that he has never tasted such food and wants to make the most of it. When Scout innocently protests against this, it is because she is shocked and does not understand Walter's poverty, but Walter is mortified. Scout has to face the wrath of Calpurnia, who teaches her about the importance of being polite to guests. Scout is still too young to really understand any of this, so she sees Calpurnia as her enemy.

After lunch, when the boys have left, Scout asks Atticus to get rid of Calpurnia but he refuses and reminds Scout that they could not function as a family without Calpurnia. We see that Atticus has great respect for his black maid, whom he trusts to raise his children; this would have been very unusual for a southern white employer in the 1930s and it shows us that Atticus is not a typical white southerner.

When Scout returns to school in the afternoon, there is more drama with Miss Caroline Fisher. Miss Fisher screams when she sees a 'cootie' crawling out of Burris Ewell's hair. She confronts Burris, who is very abusive towards her, calling her a 'snot-nosed slut of a school teacher' before leaving the classroom.

This scene in the classroom give us our first insight into the dysfunctional Ewell family. The children turn up for school on the first day every year and never come again; the truancy officer has given up on them. Burris is filthy, rude and disrespectful; the Maycomb children want nothing to do with him.

Later that evening, Atticus explains more to Scout about the Ewells and how they have been 'the disgrace of Maycomb for three generations'. Atticus also shares his wisdom with Scout, asking her to put herself in Miss Caroline's shoes, and imagine what it was like for her, being new to Maycomb and not knowing anything about the Cunninghams and the Ewells. Scout remains unimpressed by Miss Fisher, but she and Atticus reach a compromise and they agree that she may continue reading at home, and they won't say anything to Miss Fisher. This conversation shows Atticus's skill as a parent; he listens to his child, he is patient and understanding and he explains things carefully.

KEY QUOTATIONS

'Atticus said Calpurnia had more education than most coloured folks.'

'You never really understand a person until you . . . climb into his skin and walk around in it.'

'Atticus said the Ewells had been the disgrace of Maycomb for three generations. None of them had done an honest day's work in his recollection.'

'Mr Bob Ewell, Burris's father, was permitted to hunt and trap out of season.'

'. . . when a man spends his relief checks on green whiskey his children have a way of crying from hunger pains.' (Atticus)

Chapter Four

The school year passes quickly, and for Scout it is uneventful and unfulfilling. However, outside school there is some mystery and excitement for Scout and Jem. One day, Scout finds some chewing gum in a hole in a big tree outside the Radley house. Chewing gum is a rare treat. Another day, Jem and Scout find two rare lucky pennies.

Dill arrives with the summer, and the children spend their holidays 'playing Boo Radley'. This means they have endless entertainment, acting out plays about the Radley family on the street. The mysterious Radley family fascinates the children and appeals to their imagination. It never occurs to the children that somebody might be watching them. The last sentence of the chapter tells us that: 'Someone inside the [Radley] house was laughing.' The reader can only imagine who this might be.

KEY QUOTATIONS

'Some tin-foil was sticking in a knot-hole just above my eye level, winking at me in the afternoon sun.'

'Mrs Dubose was the meanest old woman who ever lived.'

'It was a melancholy little drama, woven from bits and scraps of gossip and neighbourhood legend.'

'Jem told me I was being a girl, that girls always imagined things, that's why other people hated them so, and if I started behaving like one I could just go off and find some to play with.'

'Someone inside the house was laughing.'

Chapter Five

As the summer continues, Scout often finds herself excluded from Jem and Dill's games because she is a girl. At this point in Scout's development, she deeply resents being called a girl; she is still a tomboy and often beats up Dill when he annoys her. On the plus side, she becomes closer to her neighbour, Miss Maudie, who shows the children great kindness and is regarded as a friend rather than an adult.

Miss Maudie is important in the novel because the children learn a lot from her. Like Atticus, she is a sort of mentor, and in Chapter Five she teaches Scout about the darker side of Christianity when it is in the wrong hands. For instance, the Radleys are 'foot-washing Baptists' and they believe that 'anything that's pleasure is a sin'. She also tells Scout not to believe everything she hears about Boo Radley; she remembers him as a polite young man and suggests that he may have good reasons for not wanting to come outside.

One day, the children write a note to Boo Radley, asking him to come out to meet them. Atticus catches Jem trying to send the note by a fishing pole, and they are sharply warned to leave Boo alone and stop playing the Boo Radley game. The children have to obey Atticus, but their fascination with Boo continues.

This chapter is important because it examines the attitudes of religious extremists and suggests that religion can have a very destructive effect on human relations. We see that not all people who are Christians behave in a Christian manner. The theme of religious hypocrisy will be explored later in the novel.

KEY QUOTATIONS

'You are too young to understand it . . . but sometimes the bible in the hand of one man is worse than a whiskey bottle in the hand of – oh, of your father.' (Miss Maudie)

'The things that happen to people we never really know. What happens to people behind closed doors, what secrets.' (Miss Maudie)

'Atticus Finch is the same in his house as he is on the public streets.' (Miss Maudie)

Chapter Six

As the summer draws to a close, Dill has only one night left in Maycomb and it is his last chance to try to get a look at Boo Radley. Dill, Jem and Scout wait until it's dark and then sneak up to the Radley porch to try to peep in through the window. They see a shadow on the porch and run away in terror. As they are escaping, they hear the roar of a shotgun and Jem's trousers get caught on the Radley fence.

Naturally, all the neighbours come out when they hear the gun. Miss Stephanie Crawford, the neighbourhood gossip, loves the drama and quickly adds her own touches to the story: 'Mr Radley shot a Negro in his collard patch . . . Scared him pale . . . Says if anyone sees a white nigger around, that's the one. Says he's got the other barrel waitin' for the next sound he hears in that patch, an' next time he won't aim high, be it dog, nigger or – '

Miss Stephanie's language and her account of events show just how acceptable racism was to people in Maycomb. Nobody bats an eyelid at the words she uses, or the fact that Mr Radley felt perfectly entitled to shoot a black person for entering his garden.

Jem then has to explain why he has no trousers, and Dill, who is streetwise and quick-witted, tells Atticus that they were playing strip poker. Scout and Jem don't even know what that is, but the neighbours are horrified. Worse still, Jem will have to sneak out in the night when everyone is sleeping to get his trousers back. Scout is terrified that he will be shot, but he returns safely with his trousers.

KEY QUOTATIONS

'Atticus ain't ever whipped me since I can remember. I wanta keep it that way.' (Jem)

Chapter Seven

It takes Jem a week to recover from his ordeal. He tells Scout that when he returned for his trousers, which had been tangled in the fence, they were folded over the fence waiting for him, and they had been mended by somebody. To add to the mystery, the children continue to find more treats in the knot-hole of the tree outside Radleys: a ball of twine, soap dolls which have been carved into images of Jem and Scout, a spelling medal and a pocket watch on a chain. The children are mystified by these gifts, which seem to be for them. Who is this mysterious giver of gifts? They decide to leave a thank-you note in the tree. When they return the next day, the knot-hole has been filled in with cement. They learn that Mr Nathan Radley has done this and Jem is deeply upset.

KEY QUOTATIONS

'He stood there until nightfall, and I waited for him. When we went in the house I saw he had been crying; his face was dirty in the right places, but I thought it odd that I had not heard him.'

Chapter Eight

The winter comes, Mrs Radley dies and the children see snow for the first time in their lives. The snow is a big event for all in Maycomb because it has not snowed since 1885, so the telephone operator announces that school will close for the day. The children are thrilled and play in the snow all day.

Late that night, Atticus wakes them and brings them outside. Miss Maudie's house is on fire, and all of the neighbours, along with the fire brigade, are desperately trying to put out the fire. The children watch in dismay as they stand outside the Radley house, shivering and freezing in the snow. The neighbours eventually give up trying to save Miss Maudie's home as the fire takes over.

At the end of the night, Scout is shocked to discover that someone has put a blanket around her shoulders to keep her warm. Atticus tells them it could only have been Boo. They were closer than ever to seeing Boo, and they missed the opportunity. The reader can see that Boo is constantly 'looking out' for these children who are never far from his home.

KEY QUOTATIONS

'Looks like all of Maycomb was out tonight, in one way or another.'
(Atticus)

Chapter Nine

This chapter marks an important phase in Scout's development and we also gain our first insight into Atticus's work in preparation for the big trial.

In school, Scout gets into a fight with a boy called Cecil Jacobs because he states that her 'daddy defended niggers'. When Scout talks to Atticus about this event, he gives her a calm, reasoned explanation. He will be defending a black man called Tom Robinson. Most people believe he is wrong to defend a black man, but he must obey his conscience, regardless of popular opinion. He warns Scout that she may hear 'some ugly talk' about the trial at school, and he implores her to stay out of fights. The next day at school, as Cecil Jacobs continues to insult Scout, she walks away from a fight for the first time in her life.

The Finch family spends Christmas with their relations at Aunt Alexandra's house. Scout clashes with Aunt Alexandra and compares her to Mount Everest: 'throughout my early life, she was cold and there'. Aunt Alexandra constantly finds fault with Scout; she does not approve of the way Atticus is raising her, she complains about her wearing trousers and is determined to turn Scout into a lady. Luckily for Scout, Atticus ignores Aunt Alexandra's complaints. However, Scout cannot ignore a comment from Francis, her aunt's grandson. Francis is a snob and he describes Dill as a 'little runt' who gets passed around by his many relatives. He also calls Atticus a 'nigger-lover' and says he is disgracing the family name. We see once again in the novel how most children inherit the prejudiced attitudes of their parents or grandparents. This time, Scout does not walk away from a fight; she attacks Francis.

Later that night, Scout overhears Atticus talking to Uncle Jack. She learns more about the trial – there is little hope for Tom Robinson as it is a black man's word against that of the Ewells. But most important, she learns that she and Jem will be affected by the trial. They will have to be strong, mature and brave in the coming months. Atticus hopes that his children will not catch 'Maycomb's usual disease', racism.

Until now, Scout and Jem have shared a very sheltered, innocent and carefree childhood. This chapter prepares us for the fact that all this is about to change.

KEY QUOTATIONS

'. . . every lawyer gets at least one case in his lifetime that affects him personally. This one's mine, I guess.' (Atticus)

'Try fighting with your head for a change . . . It's a good one, even if it does resist learning.' (Atticus to Scout)

'Grandma says it's bad enough he lets you all run wild, but now he's turned out a nigger-lover we'll never be able to walk the streets of Maycomb again. He's ruinin' the family, that's what he's doin'.' (Cousin Francis)

'I hope and I pray I can get Jem and Scout through it without bitterness, and most of all, without catching Maycomb's usual disease.' (Atticus)

Chapter Ten

Atticus's crucial advice, which informs the theme of the entire novel, is offered in this chapter: 'Shoot all the bluejays you want . . . but remember it's a sin to kill a mockingbird'. Atticus, the realist, knows that guns and hunting are a way of life in America and he can't stop Jem from shooting some day, but he urges him to leave the mockingbird alone. The next day, Miss Maudie explains that shooting a mockingbird is a sin because they hurt nobody; they only 'sing their hearts out for us'. Thus, the mockingbird becomes a symbol of innocence, which should not be harmed or persecuted.

Despite Atticus's wisdom, the children are embarrassed by his age: 'Atticus was feeble: he was nearly fifty.' Scout and Jem are certain he has no manly or physical accomplishments, yet they see a different side to him when he saves the town from a 'mad dog' in February.

Suspense is created in this scene by the author's description of Calpurnia's panicked reaction and the clever build-up of detail:

'"He's comin' this way."'

'Calpurnia stared, then grabbed us by the shoulders and ran us home.'

Calpurnia rings Atticus at work, then rings the operator, Eula May, and warns all the neighbours to stay inside. She even runs onto the Radley porch to warn them. It is unheard of for a black woman to do this; she is supposed to use the back door, but there is no time. The whole neighbourhood gets involved and the sheriff arrives with Atticus, carrying a rifle.

Lee's description of atmosphere is excellent:

* 'Nothing is more deadly than a deserted, waiting street.' (This sounds like a scene from a western – a showdown between two cowboys!)
* 'I haven't shot a gun in thirty years.' (Atticus)
* 'He walked quickly, but I thought he moved like an underwater swimmer; time had slowed to a nauseating crawl.'

When Atticus shoots the dog and saves the town, Scout and Jem see their father in a new light. They learn that he is 'the deadest shot in Maycomb'. The children are left in awe of their father and they realise that there can be much more to a person than meets the eye. Miss Maudie also continues to act as a mentor, and helps the children to understand Atticus's complexity and his pacifism: 'I think maybe he put his gun down when he realized that God had given him an unfair advantage over most living things. I guess he decided he wouldn't shoot till he had to, and he had to today.' As a result of Miss Maudie's words, the children continue to grow in awareness.

Students should pay attention to how this chapter is written: it is an excellent example of storytelling skill.

KEY QUOTATIONS

'Shoot all the bluejays you want . . . but remember it's a sin to kill a mockingbird.' (Atticus)

'He walked quickly, but I thought he moved like an underwater swimmer; time had slowed to a nauseating crawl.' (Scout)

Chapter Eleven

This chapter tells the story of the infamous Mrs Dubose. Mrs Dubose is feared and hated by Jem and Scout. Every day as the children walk past her house, she screams abuse at them. But one day, she goes too far when she insults their mother's memory and says, 'Your father's no better than the niggers and trash he works for.' The children are shocked because they have become used to insults from other children, but this is the first time an adult has insulted them in this way. In a fit of temper, Jem vandalises her garden, destroying her flowers (camellias) with a baton he had bought for Scout.

Naturally, Jem has to be punished for this. Atticus is horrified at what he has done to an old lady, and once Jem has cleaned up her garden, he is told he will have to go and read to her every day after school for a month. This is a very harsh punishment because the children are terrified of Mrs Dubose, whose house is 'dark and creepy', and they are sure she carries a pistol under her shawls. As awful as this punishment is, Scout accompanies Jem without hesitation. This shows us that, despite their differences, Jem and Scout are very close and will support each other through tough times.

Reading to Mrs Dubose every day is a strange and unpleasant experience for the children. Her maid sets a clock every day, there is a syringe near her bed and she drools and falls asleep quickly. The first session ends very quickly, but each day the sessions get a little bit longer. When the month is up, Atticus makes Jem continue for another week.

When Mrs Dubose dies, Atticus tells the children that Mrs Dubose was the bravest person he ever knew. She was a morphine addict and this explained her fits of abuse at passers-by; she could not be blamed for her behaviour, but she was determined to kick the habit before she died and the children unwittingly helped her to do this. Once more, the children have grown in awareness and learnt more about the complexity and mystery of human beings.

KEY QUOTATIONS

'Jem and I hated her.' (Scout)

'This case, Tom Robinson's case, is something that goes to the essence of a man's conscience – Scout, I couldn't go to church and worship God if I didn't try to help that man.' (Atticus)

'. . . before I can live with other folks I've got to live with myself.' (Atticus)

'I wanted you to see what real courage is, instead of getting the idea that courage is a man with a gun in his hand. It's when you know you're licked before you begin but you begin anyway and you see it through no matter what.' (Atticus)

'She was the bravest person I ever knew.' (Atticus)

Part Two

The focus of Part Two is on the events surrounding Tom Robinson's trial and the trial itself. The children are forced to grow up fast, they face real danger on numerous occasions and they have to come to terms with some ugly aspects of human nature.

Chapter Twelve

Jem is now twelve and he becomes moody and distant. In true southern tradition, Calpurnia starts to call him 'Mister Jem'. Scout is lonelier than ever without him or Dill for company, and she becomes closer to Calpurnia. Scout's relationship with Cal has softened and this shows that Scout is maturing; the epic war with Cal is over and Cal is now a role model and an ally for Scout, who is slowly learning to accept her own femininity.

The children see a cartoon of their father being ridiculed in the *Montgomery Advertiser*. Jem believes it shows that Atticus is doing the jobs that no one else wants to do. It also shows the reader that the trial is big news outside Maycomb. Atticus is doing something groundbreaking and historic.

One Sunday, the children attend Calpurnia's church, as their father is away and she can't take them to a white church. The church is called 'First Purchase' because it was paid for with the first earnings of freed slaves. Visiting the black church is like stepping into another world for the children – quite an adventure in a racially segregated society. Even Calpurnia's speech is different among her people, 'she was talking like the rest of them'. The children are formally welcomed by Reverend Sykes and treated as very special guests. We learn that there are no bibles here, as most of the black community can't read. Calpurnia is very unusual as a black person who can read; she was taught by Miss Maudie's aunt. Again, we are reminded of the importance of education in the novel.

KEY QUOTATIONS

'She [Calpurnia] seemed glad to see me when I appeared in the kitchen, and by watching her I began to think there was some skill involved in being a girl.'

'She was talking like the rest of them.'

Chapter Thirteen

The role of 'feminine influence' is explored in this chapter. To Scout's horror, Aunt Alexandra has come to turn Scout into a lady and to 'arrange, advise, caution, and warn'. She believes Scout has no 'feminine influence' in the home, as she does not count Calpurnia as a role model or as a significant woman.

Aunt Alexandra represents the 'fine folks' of Maycomb, is clearly a snob and 'an incurable gossip'. As a result, Maycomb welcomes her. Through Aunt Alexandra's presence, we learn more about Maycomb's caste system, the preoccupation with family background and how people are quickly judged and labelled according to their family history. If someone does something wrong, it is quickly blamed on their family genes. People are very narrow-minded, and fearful of new people, new ideas, anything different. The link between fear and ignorance is made clear. Aunt Alexandra's values clash with those of Atticus, but they bring the reality of the southern outlook into the children's home.

> ## KEY QUOTATIONS
>
> 'Aunt Alexandra was of the opinion . . . that the longer a family had been squatting on a patch of land the finer it was.'
>
> '[Maycomb] remained the same size for a hundred years, an island in a patchwork sea of cotton fields and timber land . . . It grew inward.'
>
> 'Aunt Alexandra fitted into the world of Maycomb like a hand into a glove, but never into the world of Jem and me.'

Chapter Fourteen

The people of Maycomb continue to point fingers at Scout and Jem, disagreements with Aunt Alexandra continue at home and Jem tries to assert his authority over Scout. As usual, Scout fights back to show him that 'We were still equals'. Aunt Alexandra also clashes with Atticus when he refuses to dismiss Calpurnia, whom he regards as family. The highlight of this chapter, however, is the appearance of Dill as a 'filthy brown package' under Scout's bed. Dill has run away from his mother and 'new father' and has made it all the way to Maycomb alone. Jem shows his sense of responsibility by immediately telling Atticus about Dill, so that Dill's family can be told of his whereabouts.

> ## KEY QUOTATIONS
>
> 'Alexandra, Calpurnia's not leaving this house until she wants to . . . She's a faithful member of this family.' (Atticus)

Chapter Fifteen

It is decided that Dill can stay in Maycomb. The night before the trial, Sheriff Heck Tate visits Atticus to warn him about the 'Old Sarum bunch', a gang of white men who have been threatening to take the law into their own hands. Because of their racism and ignorance, this gang does not want Tom to have his day in court where he will be defended like a white man. This creates tension, with an awareness of the danger and potential for violence surrounding the trial.

Late at night, Jem, Scout and Dill follow Atticus and find him guarding the jail where Tom Robinson is being held. The following details create suspense:

- The whole square is deserted until 'four dusty cars came in from the Meridian highway, moving slowly in a line.'
- 'He seemed to be expecting them.'
- The appearance of the men is eerie and the contrast between light and darkness is dramatic: 'Shadows became substance as light revealed solid shapes moving towards the jail door.'
- The men inform Atticus that the sheriff has been called out on 'a snipe hunt' and will be away in the woods all night. Atticus is deserted and the sense of danger is very real and immediate.
- 'There was a smell of stale whiskey and pig-pen about, and when I glanced around I discovered that these men were strangers . . . I began to feel sweat gathering at the edges of my hair; I could stand anything but a bunch of people looking at me.'

Scout sees Mr Cunningham and, regarding him as a family friend, asks him lots of personal questions about Walter. The tension is broken when Mr Cunningham responds to Scout, and the men leave. However, the seriousness of the situation is underlined when Mr Underwood, the editor of the *Maycomb Tribune*, is seen leaning out of his window with his shotgun: 'Had you covered all the time, Atticus.' This shows the reader that the threat of violence was not imagined by the children; it was very real.

KEY QUOTATIONS

'A nightmare was upon us.'

Chapter Sixteen

Following the incident with the Old Sarum bunch, Atticus explains to Scout and Jem how they influenced the mob and caused them to leave:

KEY QUOTATIONS

'A mob's always made up of people . . . a gang of wild animals can be stopped, simply because they're human . . . you children last night made Walter Cunningham stand in my shoes for a minute.'

This is a fine example of Atticus's philosophy being put into practice, and it shows his unshakeable belief in the goodness in humanity; he always sees the best in people.

The next day, all of Maycomb turns up for Tom Robinson's trial, regarding it as 'a gala occasion'. For the white community, the event is a day out and an excuse for a great picnic. It is clear that the white people are hungry for the entertainment and drama of the trial. While all these people claim to be Christian, we see that their different versions of Christianity cause more divisions than unity: for instance, the foot-washing Baptists continue to hurl abuse at Miss Maudie, who cheerfully defies them.

An interesting character emerges in this scene: Mr Dolphus Raymond. He is a rich white man who has had several children with a black woman, and he spends all his time with black people. He gets away with this scandalous behavior because he is rich, he comes from a 'real old family' and people assume he is always drunk. It is widely believed that he drinks whiskey from a Coca-Cola bottle. His children are isolated by both the black and the white community because they are racially mixed, and it is believed he has sent two of his grown children up north where they will be accepted. Once more, the hypocrisy of this supposedly Christian society is evident.

Unknown to Atticus, the children sneak into the courtroom to watch the trial.

Chapter Seventeen

This chapter builds a picture of the Ewells and the way they live. It is clear that they are ignorant, deprived people on the outer margins of society. The only advantage they have over black people is that, underneath all the dirt, their skin is white:

- '. . . people like the Ewells lived as guests of the county in prosperity as well as in the depths of a depression.'
- They were known for their 'congenital defects, various worms and the diseases indigenous to filthy surroundings'.
- 'Maycomb's Ewells lived behind the town garbage dump in what was once a negro cabin . . . Nobody was quite sure how many children were on the place.'

During this chapter, Mr Ewell testifies. He claims that he came home, found Tom assaulting Mayella, and Tom escaped, leaving Mayella badly beaten. His language is vulgar and his story is vague, yet the following facts emerge during his testimony:

- He did not call a doctor for Mayella.
- The right side of Mayella's face was badly bruised.
- Mr Ewell is left-handed.

KEY QUOTATIONS

'Atticus was trying to show, it seemed to me, that Mr Ewell could have beaten up Mayella.'

Chapter Eighteen

Mayella gives her testimony. In his questioning of Mayella, 'Atticus was quietly building up before the jury a picture of the Ewells' home life.' Atticus cleverly shows the jury that Mayella is a desperately lonely, isolated girl with nothing to look forward to in life.

Mayella is insulted when Atticus calls her 'ma'am'. She thinks he is mocking her as she has never been spoken to politely in her life. Like her father, she gives a vague account of events and then refuses to say another word. She does admit, though, that it was she who asked Tom Robinson to come into the house and break up a 'chiffarobe' for her.

KEY QUOTATIONS

'What did your father see in the window, the crime of rape or the best defence to it? Why don't you tell the truth, child? Didn't Bob Ewell beat you up?'

Chapter Nineteen

Tom Robinson gives his testimony. One vital fact is in his favour: as the result of an injury in his past, his left hand is useless, so he could not have beaten Mayella on the right side of her face.

Listening to Tom, Scout realises that:

> 'Mayella Ewell must have been the loneliest person in the world. She was even lonelier than Boo Radley . . . white people wouldn't have anything to do with her because she lived among pigs; Negroes wouldn't have anything to do with her because she was white.'

The hypocrisy of a Christian society is revealed once more in people's attitudes towards the Ewells: 'Maycomb gave them Christmas baskets, welfare money, and the back of its hand'. People want to be seen to be charitable, but ultimately they do not want to be reminded that people like the Ewells exist. It embarrasses the community of Maycomb that white people could fall so low as to be more deprived than the black community.

Tom's version of events is very different from the Ewells'. His is very precise and detailed. He claims that Mayella frequently asked for his help around the house. On the day of the alleged rape, she called him in, informed him that she had sent all the children away and then tried to kiss him. Bob Ewell came home, looked in the window and saw her trying to kiss Tom. He roared, 'You god-damn whore, I'll kill ya,' and Tom saw no option but to run for his life.

Tom makes one fatal mistake in his testimony: under cross-examination by Mr Gilmer, he tells the court that he helped Mayella out on a regular basis because he felt sorry for her. This is unacceptable to the jury – they could never believe or accept that a black man could feel sorry for a white woman. The jury, like most white southerners of the time, believe that even the 'white trash' were superior to black people and that no white people could fall lower on the social scale than 'Negroes'. It is offensive to a deeply racist southern jury that Tom could claim to have felt sorry for a white woman, and they will not forgive him for this.

Upset by Mr Gilmer's treatment of Tom, Dill breaks down and Scout has to take him outside.

KEY QUOTATIONS

'But the damage was done. Below us, nobody liked Tom Robinson's answer.'

Chapter Twenty

Dill and Scout meet Mr Dolphus Raymond, in a scene that offers some light relief from the intensity of the trial. Scout has always believed the rumours that Mr Dolphus Raymond is an 'evil man', but she is fascinated by him. Once more, she learns that she has misjudged somebody and been fooled by appearances. Mr Dolphus explains that he only pretends to be drunk all the time, so that people will ignore his lifestyle. He is an amusing, kind and humane character. He analyses the difference between children and adults: Dill is still a child so he cries 'about the simple hell people give other people'; but Mr Dolphus points out the sad and painful truth that Dill, like all children, will grow up, life will harden him and he won't cry about injustice or racism.

The scene with Mr Dolphus is important as it allows the reader time to stop and digest all that has happened in court and to pause and reflect on the novel's central themes – racism, injustice, childhood and innocence, growing up and coming to terms with the world.

Back in court, Atticus gives his closing speech to the jury and tries to make them understand Mayella's position, and why she is accusing Tom:

'She is the victim of cruel poverty and ignorance, but I cannot pity her: she is white . . . She tempted a Negro. She did something that in our society is unspeakable: she kissed a black man . . . No code mattered to her before she broke it, but it came crashing down on her afterwards.'

He also reminds the jury that there is 'not one iota of medical evidence' that Tom assaulted Mayella.

Chapter Twenty-One

While the jury retires to make its decision, Jem is excited and can't wait for the verdict. Based on the evidence given in court, it seems impossible that the jury could return a guilty verdict; after all, Tom would face the death penalty if they convicted him. The Ewells have made fools of themselves and there is no medical evidence whatsoever. We see the child in Jem: in his belief in justice and his certainty that people will do the right thing. This confidence in humanity is shattered when the jury returns its guilty verdict.

As Atticus leaves the court, the black community gives him a standing ovation, bringing the trial to a dramatic and powerful close.

KEY QUOTATIONS

'A jury never looks at a defendant it has convicted, and when this jury came in, not one of them looked at Tom Robinson.'

Chapter Twenty-Two

The day after the trial, Atticus assures the children that there will be an appeal. Miss Maudie steps in to comfort the children and help them come to terms with the outcome. Jem is utterly disillusioned with the people of Maycomb, whom he always believed to be 'the best folks in the world', but Miss Maudie reminds him that some people do actually care about Tom Robinson.

Bob Ewell approaches Atticus on the street, spits on his face and says 'he'd get him if it took the rest of his life'.

KEY QUOTATIONS

'We're so rarely called on to be Christians, but when we are, we've got men like Atticus to go for us.' (Miss Maudie)

Chapter Twenty-Three

The children are disturbed by Bob Ewell's threat, but Atticus dismisses it – he thinks it's just talk.

As the summer passes, Tom Robinson remains in prison and waits while the higher court reviews his case. If he loses his appeal, he faces the electric chair. As Jem begins to lose faith in juries and the entire legal system, Atticus explains the benefits of their legal system, as well as its drawbacks. Even though the jury convicted Tom, they had a hard time convincing one of the Cunninghams to convict. This shows that the trial was not a waste of time – attitudes are slowly changing because of it. Nonetheless, Aunt Alexandra does not want Scout associating with Walter Cunningham or his kind. She is firm and determined in her snobbery: 'Finch women aren't interested in that sort of people.' Not satisfied with this answer, Scout presses Aunt Alexandra for the real reason why she can't be friends with Walter Cunningham and Aunt Alexandra's final reply is harsh: 'Because – he – is – trash, that's why you can't play with him.'

Later, Jem and Scout analyse Aunt Alexandra's obsession with 'fine folks'. They discuss all the different kinds of 'folks' in Maycomb, but Scout comes to the conclusion that there's 'just one kind of folks. Folks.' This is a positive moment because it shows that the children can think for themselves and choose to reject Maycomb's caste system.

Tom Robinson's trial has forced the children to grow in wisdom and understanding, and they have grown out of their obsession with Boo Radley. In fact, it has made them understand him more.

KEY QUOTATIONS

'I think I'm beginning to understand why Boo Radley's stayed shut up in the house all this time . . . it's because he wants to stay inside.' (Jem)

Chapter Twenty-Four
This chapter focuses very closely on the religious hypocrisy that has been simmering beneath Maycomb's Christian surface for so long. Aunt Alexandra is hosting a missionary tea, and Scout is expected to wear a dress and help with refreshments.

The ladies who meet are supposed to be united by Christian charity and a desire to help the missionaries to spread Christianity. Mrs Merriweather does most of the talking and, despite her jolly-sounding name, her tone is malicious. She regards herself as 'the most devout lady in Maycomb'. Like most supporters of the Christian missions in the 1930s, she believes that the tribes being converted in Africa are mere savages. Her attitude towards the 'heathens' is patronising and deeply racist. She represents an arrogant sort of Christian who never misses an opportunity to preach to others.

The conversation that takes place here shows that the trial has failed to change the opinions of the ladies; if anything, it has made them worse. They are annoyed that Atticus has stirred up discontent among the black servants. They describe their servants as 'sulky' and 'dissatisfied' after the trial, and Mrs Merriweather has even threatened to sack her maid if she doesn't change her mood. Their lack of sympathy is decidedly unchristian and merely emphasises their hypocrisy. Scout is mystified by the way the women communicate, blending polite language and genteel manners with snide remarks and put-downs. She reflects that she is more happy in the world of men, but she can adapt to the world of women and behave like a lady when she has to. This is important for Scout's development: she is coming to terms with her femininity and learning to accept it.

The meeting is interrupted by the terrible news that Tom Robinson has been shot dead while trying to escape prison.

KEY QUOTATIONS

'I wondered at this world of women . . . There was no doubt about it, I must soon enter this world, where on its surface fragrant ladies rocked slowly, fanned gently, and drank cool water.'

Chapter Twenty-Five

Word gets out that Tom is dead. There is little sympathy for him among the white community: 'To Maycomb, Tom's death was typical. Typical of a nigger to cut and run.' Mr Ewell continues to threaten his enemies.

KEY QUOTATIONS

'Tom was a dead man the minute Mayella Ewell opened her mouth and screamed.'

Chapter Twenty-Six

The children go back to school, they mature and time passes. Scout still thinks of Boo from time to time and, while she no longer fears him, she still wonders if she will ever see him: 'I expressed a stray desire just to have one good look at Boo Radley before I died.' Like Jem, Scout struggles to understand humanity and becomes philosophical: 'I came to the conclusion that people were just peculiar. I withdrew from them, and never thought about them until I was forced to.'

For the first time in the novel, there is a reference to the wider world when the teacher tells the children about Hitler and his persecution of the Jews. Class and teacher openly discuss prejudice without any mention of the racial prejudice in their own society. Afterwards, Scout hears her teacher gossiping with Miss Stephanie and making racist comments about black people.

The mention of Hitler in the novel reminds the reader that time is passing and the world is about to change. Persecution of one race will not be tolerated forever. (Remember: the novel was set in the 1930s, but written in the 1950s, after World War II.)

KEY QUOTATIONS

'Over here we don't believe in persecuting anybody. Persecution comes from people who are prejudiced.' (Miss Gates, teacher)

Chapter Twenty-Seven

Life goes on, but Bob Ewell continues to make threats. He is sacked from unpaid employment for the WPA (Works Progress Administration) and he publicly blames Atticus for this. One night, Judge Taylor spots a shadow near his house and he fetches his shotgun in order to guard his house. On another occasion, Bob Ewell follows Helen Robinson (Tom's wife) home, muttering obscenities at her from behind. He is clearly a bully bent on revenge and this prepares us for what he does in the next chapter, the novel's climax.

Chapter Twenty-Eight

This chapter is another fine example of Harper Lee's storytelling skill; the atmosphere of suspense and fear makes for compelling reading.

The children attend the Hallowe'en pageant at school, with Scout dressed up as a ham! Being wrapped up in chicken wire makes Scout's movements awkward and restricted. On their way home in the dark, Scout and Jem sense that they are being followed. The description of the presence behind them is eerie and threatening. Suddenly they are attacked in the dark. There is much confusion as the children can see nothing during this frenzied attack. Scout's costume saves her from being stabbed, as the attacker cannot cut through the chicken wire. Jem is attacked and falls in the dark. Amidst the panic, Scout realises that there is another person there in the dark, a person who grabs their attacker and saves their lives.

This figure carries Jem home and Scout follows, leaving the mystery attacker on the ground under the tree. Once the children are home, Atticus sends for the doctor and the sheriff. Jem has broken his arm, but otherwise the children are fine. By the end of the chapter, the children's attacker is revealed: Bob Ewell is lying dead under the tree with a knife in his ribs.

KEY QUOTATIONS

'It was slowly coming to me that there were now four people under the tree.'

Chapter Twenty-Nine

While Jem sleeps after his ordeal, the mysterious Boo is finally revealed and Scout's wish is fulfilled. Her face-to-face encounter with Boo is a revelation and she is moved to tears. She has come a long way since the childish games and fascination with Boo. The real Boo is no phantom, just a 'sickly . . . delicate . . . timid' man who is afraid of the light. Scout sees the mockingbird where once she only imagined a monster.

KEY QUOTATIONS

'They were white hands, sickly white hands that had never seen the sun, so white they stood out garishly against the dull cream wall . . . His face was as white as his hands, but for a shadow on his jutting chin . . . His lips parted into a timid smile, and our neighbour's image blurred with my sudden tears.

'"Hey Boo," I said.'

Chapter Thirty

Atticus and Sheriff Heck Tate retrace the night's events. Atticus needs to be sure that Jem did not stab Bob Ewell. Heck Tate insists that Jem did not stab Ewell, that he actually fell on his own knife. He was drunk, after all. It is never said, but it is understood, that Boo is responsible for Ewell's death. They agree that no one in the neighbourhood should be told that Boo saved the children's lives; Boo does not deserve to be dragged into the limelight, as he could never cope with all the attention. Boo is an innocent who deserves to be protected. Atticus thanks Boo for saving his children.

KEY QUOTATIONS

'Well, it'd be sort of like shootin' a mockingbird, wouldn't it?' (Scout)

Chapter Thirty-One

In a touching gesture of friendship and appreciation, Scout takes Boo by the hand and walks him home. Standing on the Radley porch, she realises that Boo would have seen the children growing up from his window. She reflects on the summers spent with Dill, playing Boo Radley and trying to make Boo come out. Boo was watching all along. It was Boo they had heard laughing on the porch, Boo who had sewn up Jem's trousers, covered Scout with a blanket during the snow and left gifts for them in the tree. Now, more than ever, she understands Atticus's wisdom:

> 'Atticus was right. One time he said you never really know a man until you stand in his shoes and walk around in them. Just standing on the Radley porch was enough.'

Finally, as the novel draws to a close, Scout says she 'felt very old'. But, of course, we are reminded that she is still young and innocent, if only because she believes 'there wasn't much else for us to learn, except possibly algebra'.

KEY QUOTATIONS

'Boo was our neighbour. He gave us two soap dolls, a broken watch and chain, a pair of good-luck pennies, and our lives. But neighbours give in return. We never put back into the tree what we took out of it: we had given him nothing, and it made me sad.'

4. Character Analysis

Scout

Jean Louise Finch, or Scout, is the novel's narrator and principal character. She is a unique and remarkable character who does not quite fit in, or do what is expected of young girls (or Finch ladies) in 1930s Alabama. Readers will note that Scout at the end of the novel is very different from Scout at the beginning, and this is because she has developed so much as a character.

At the start of the novel, she is a determined, spirited tomboy; she loves to play with the boys and fight with the boys. She shocks her neighbours by wearing trousers. She spends most of her time with Jem, her brother, and Dill, her friend who visits every summer. She can't bear to be reminded that she is a girl and she is often excluded from the boys' games because she is a girl. At times, being a girl makes her very lonely – she has no mother, sisters or female friends of her own age. She tries to solve all problems by fighting and it takes her a long time to follow her father's advice and learn to fight with her head instead of her fists. Her bad temper is possibly her greatest flaw.

She also stands out from the crowd because she is very clever. She can read the newspaper before she starts school and she can't even remember starting to read or being taught to read. Her knowledge of the law is remarkable for her age.

She is also outspoken, and this gets her into trouble with Miss Caroline on her first day at school. Her big mouth often makes her insensitive. For instance, she loves Dill but openly challenges him when he lies about his 'father'. She does not have the maturity or sensitivity to stay quiet and let Dill pretend.

She is stubborn and strong-willed, and this means she clashes with people who have authority over her – Calpurnia, Miss Caroline, Aunt Alexandra. She does not disobey her father, but she certainly challenges him and tries to get around him. However, Atticus always gets around her in the end.

Scout grows and develops immensely in the course of the novel. Early in the novel, she believes all the rumours that she hears around Maycomb and picks up many of Maycomb's attitudes – Boo is a phantom, Mr Dolphus Raymond is evil, black people are only 'niggers' and Atticus should not defend them. Atticus tries to teach her to overcome these prejudices and to be less judgemental of others, but she really learns these lessons from lived experiences and encounters with people like Mrs Dubose, Mayella Ewell, Mr Dolphus Raymond, Mr Cunningham, Boo Radley. All these characters were easily misjudged, yet Scout learned to see beyond appearances, to crawl inside their skin and see things from their perspective. This makes her a very wise child by the end of the novel.

She also learns to become more accepting of her femininity. For some, it may seem that she gives into Aunt Alexandra's pressure to be a lady, but it could also be said that she adapts and becomes more flexible. She learns that there are times when she has to act like a traditional southern lady if she is to be involved in the 'world of women', and she accepts this compromise, while staying involved and happy in the world of men.

In the final chapter, we see that the rebellious little tomboy who fights with her fists has made way for a thoughtful, wise, mature and experienced young lady.

Jem

Jem Finch, Scout's older brother by four years, is always a little wiser and more mature than Scout. He advises and guides Scout, explains things to her when he can and tries to keep her out of fights. They play together a lot, but he has his boundaries; he frequently abandons her when Dill is around, and she is not allowed to play with him in the school yard.

Being older than Scout, he is more tactful and understanding of people's situations. For instance, he stops Scout from beating up Walter Cunningham and then invites Walter home for dinner. He also senses that Dill invents all kinds of fantasies because something is missing from his own life. Jem is mature and sensitive enough to pretend he believes Dill and he tries to stop Scout from ridiculing him. He is an important role model for Scout, pointing her in the right direction when he can.

Despite his maturity, Jem is still a carefree, innocent child for much of the novel. Like Scout, he believes all the rumours about Boo Radley. He also craves excitement and can't refuse a dare, which is why he goes up to the Radley porch when Dill dares him. He often teases Scout for being a girl and uses this to insult her when she annoys him. When he reaches puberty, Scout finds him moody, distant and unbearable. He also becomes bossy.

Like Scout, Jem is very intelligent and is strongly influenced by his father, Atticus. His understanding of the law is even better than Scout's as he is four years her senior. His relationship with his father is very important to him. He wants to be a lawyer and a gentleman, just like Atticus. He hates to disappoint Atticus; when he leaves his trousers tangled in Boo Radley's fence he has to retrieve them so that Atticus does not find out that he was the one in the Radleys' garden. He says Atticus has never whipped him and he wants to keep it that way; in other words, he has Atticus's approval and he wants to keep it.

Jem is compassionate and sensitive, so at times he is deeply upset by his experiences. He is badly shaken for a week after he gets his trousers back from the Radley garden and he cries alone when Mr Nathan Radley fills the tree hole with cement. He does not normally lose his temper or resort to violence, but when Mrs Dubose insults Atticus as well as the entire family, he slashes her camellias in an act of rampant vandalism. As time passes, he becomes much more mature and responsible. When Dill runs away from home, Jem tells Atticus immediately so that Dill's parents can be informed that he is safe. Scout and Dill are disgusted with him, but Jem sees the situation from an adult's rather than a child's perspective.

When Tom Robinson is found guilty, Jem is shocked by the jury's verdict. This leaves him very disillusioned with people, especially the people of Maycomb, whom he once thought were 'the best folks in the world'. Jem's experiences could make him bitter and cynical, but this does not happen, because Atticus keeps reminding him of the goodness in people and the strengths of their legal system. Ultimately, Jem learns from his experiences and becomes a wise and mature young man.

Atticus

Atticus is an educated, hard-working single parent. His wife died when his children were both very small. He is a unique individual, standing out from the crowd for many reasons.

Living in Alabama in the 1930s, he is an unusual kind of parent. He does not believe in lying to his children when they ask difficult questions; instead he explains things logically in words that they will understand. He is wise and acts as a mentor and role model to his children.

He is both strict and laid-back as a parent. He is strict about the things that matter: he has high expectations of his children; he orders them to leave Boo

Radley alone; he makes Jem pay for his attack on Mrs Dubose's garden, he does not allow them to use racist language; he insists that they treat all people with respect. However, he is laid-back about things that would scandalise his neighbours: Scout is allowed to wear trousers; he lets her play with boys; and the children call him by his first name. These things are important to Aunt Alexandra, who represents the conservative, narrow-minded outlook of Maycomb, but Atticus regards them as trivial. His attitudes are radical, considering the world he lives in.

He takes his role as a father very seriously; he says that one of the reasons he takes on Tom Robinson's trial is that he could not ever tell his children what to do if he did not obey his conscience and represent Tom in court. Unlike most people in Maycomb, he is not a hypocrite. This is why Miss Maudie admires him so much, and why she says he is the same in his house as he is on the streets.

His values are very different from those of his community. He is completely opposed to racism, which he sees as 'Maycomb's usual disease'. In Maycomb, racism is the norm, and segregation is the law: black and white people must attend separate schools and churches, black people may not vote or be members of a jury, black people are still seen as slaves and nobody minds when people openly refer to them as 'niggers' or 'darkies'. Yet Atticus treats his black maid, Calpurnia (Cal), as a faithful member of the family. He does not mind that his children attend First Purchase, the all-black church, with Calpurnia. He takes huge risks when he defends Tom Robinson; he refuses to give in to the Old Sarum bunch; he carries on knowing that the whole town is against him and his children will be bullied at school. He believes in equality in general – he welcomes Walter Cunningham to his home and respects his family, even though Aunt Alexandra believes the Cunninghams are 'trash'.

Atticus is also different because he is a pacifist – he is opposed to violence. He is the 'deadest shot in Maycomb', yet he never uses his skill with guns in a society where hunting and shooting are a part of everyday life. He constantly encourages Scout to fight with her head and not her fists.

Atticus's sense of humour adds to his appeal as a character. He often makes little jokes which the reader understands even though Scout doesn't. His good-humoured banter with Miss Maudie also reveals a man who can take a joke.

Atticus's flaw is his naivety; he always sees the good in people, trying to see things from their perspective, but sometimes he is not realistic. This is evident when he underestimates the threat of Bob Ewell. Atticus thinks that Bob Ewell is making empty threats: he won't actually do anything dangerous. Judge Taylor senses danger, Helen Robinson's employer warns him to leave Helen alone and the children are afraid, but Atticus dismisses their fears because he cannot imagine what Ewell is capable of. If it weren't for Boo Radley, the children would have lost their lives to Bob Ewell, who was determined to get revenge on Atticus.

WORDS OF WISDOM FROM ATTICUS

'You never really understand a person until you consider things from his point of view . . . until you climb into his skin and walk around in it.'

'Shoot all the bluejays you want . . . but remember it's a sin to kill a mockingbird.'

'This case, Tom Robinson's case, is something that goes to the essence of a man's conscience – Scout, I couldn't go to church and worship God if I didn't try to help that man.'

'. . . before I can live with other folks I've got to live with myself.'

'I wanted you to see what real courage is, instead of getting the idea that courage is a man with a gun in his hand. It's when you know you're licked before you begin but you begin anyway and you see it through no matter what.'

'A mob's always made up of people . . . a gang of wild animals can be stopped, simply because they're human'.

Boo Radley

Arthur Radley (Boo) is the children's mysterious neighbour who never leaves his house. Boo is a true mockingbird figure – a figure of innocence who has harmed no one and does not deserve to be persecuted. Like the mockingbird who does nothing but make beautiful music, Boo only contributes good things to the children's lives.

Boo is a victim of a strict, cruel father. He has been punished all his adult life for disgracing the family name as a young man, and the reader finds clues that he has been abused – mentally or otherwise – by his father. Mr Radley is described as 'ramrod straight', and this suggests a man who is rigid and hard. Atticus implies that Boo's father has turned him into a ghost of a man and

Calpurnia mutters that Mr Radley, Boo's father, was the 'meanest man ever God drew breath into'. He must have been very harsh indeed to make Calpurnia comment on the ways of a white person. These clues about Mr Radley make the reader more sympathetic towards Boo, who clearly came from a troubled home.

Boo is also the victim of ignorance, rumours and prejudice in the neighbourhood. People like Miss Stephanie Crawford have turned Boo into a monster and an object of terror among the people of Maycomb. People believe that he eats live squirrels and cats, that he tried to kill his father, that pecans from his garden are poisonous and that he spies on women at night. Everything that goes wrong in Maycomb or that is feared by people can be blamed on Boo:

> 'When people's azaleas froze in a cold snap, it was because he had breathed on them. Any stealthy crimes committed in Maycomb were his work.'

The children cannot be blamed for believing these stories and being prejudiced towards the 'malevolent phantom'. The rumours about Boo that circulate show that the people of Maycomb are gullible and superstitious; they also show that people in Maycomb don't have a great deal to talk about.

Yet everything that Boo contributes to the story shows his kindness and his fondness for the children. An alert reader can see that he is actually involved in their lives from a distance, rather like a guardian angel watching over them. This makes it believable when he becomes the hero of the story and saves their lives.

Why, you might ask, does Boo do so much for the children? Why should he care so much for them? The answers to these questions come to Scout in the final chapter when she stands on Boo's porch. Boo spent his time alone watching charming and innocent children playing in full view of his house, and since these children were the only entertainment and light in his life, he came to care for them. He enjoyed their fun and games, laughing at them when they played 'Boo Radley'; he had fun sending them gifts in the knot-hole of the tree until his brother found out and filled the hole with cement. He liked to take care of them – patching up Jem's trousers and leaving them on the fence, covering Scout with a blanket during the cold snap. All these actions show us a kind and caring individual. His final act of heroism and his appearance in Scout's home as a timid, fragile character prove Atticus's philosophy – it is very wrong to judge someone without walking in their shoes for a while; and it would indeed be a sin to kill a mockingbird.

Mr Radley

Mr Radley is harsh and rigid, as indicated by his appearance – he is a thin, leathery man with sharp features, and his posture is 'ramrod straight'. Like all his family, he is private and keeps to himself. He is a cruel disciplinarian who turns his son into a 'ghost' of his former self. No one knows exactly what he has done to Boo, but it is clear that Boo has been permanently damaged by his father. Calpurnia describes him as 'the meanest man'.

Mr Nathan Radley

Mr Nathan Radley is said to be the exact same as his father, so we can assume that he too is cruel and harsh. He is also detached and aloof. When he finds out that Boo has been leaving gifts in the tree-hole, his reaction is swift and final – he puts an end to this innocent activity by filling up the hole with cement. When he hears the children trespassing on his land at night, he shoots at what he believes to be an intruder and a 'nigger'.

Calpurnia

Calpurnia, the Finches' black maid, is a mother figure to Scout. Early in the novel, Scout sees her as the enemy because she is so strict and firm with her, but Atticus regards her as part of the family and he trusts her to raise his children as well as he would himself.

Calpurnia is unusual for a black person in 1930s Alabama because she can read and write, which she achieved with the help and encouragement of charitable white people (Miss Maudie's aunt, Atticus's father). The children realise how unusual she is when they visit her church, First Purchase, as Calpurnia's speech changes when she is with her own people. When Calpurnia is with the Finches, she speaks like a white person and her grammar is excellent, but when she is with her black friends and family, she speaks as they do; Scout refers to this accent as 'nigger talk'. Calpurnia explains to the children that if she spoke 'better' English among her own people she would stand out too much and people would think she was showing off. She does not use her education to impress people or act in a superior manner. Scout is very impressed that Cal has 'command of two languages' but she also wonders at her 'modest double life'.

As Scout matures, her relationship with Calpurnia blossoms and she comes to value Cal just as much as Atticus does. Cal loves the children and shows Scout great kindness and affection. She is both a mother figure for Scout, and a companion when the boys refuse to play with her.

Miss Maudie Atkinson

Miss Maudie is a mentor and friend to the children. She is a very positive influence in the children's lives; she tells them to ignore the rumours about Boo Radley – she remembers him as a polite young man who may have good reasons for not wanting to come outside. She also helps them to understand and appreciate Atticus. The reader learns a lot about Atticus and his beliefs through Miss Maudie. For instance, she is the one who explains that he is the 'deadest shot in Maycomb', but she also explains why he hates to use guns. Her admiration of Atticus increases the reader's admiration of him.

She loves nature and regards time spent indoors as a waste. She has a positive outlook on life and this is seen when her house burns down and she insists on looking on the bright side of the situation. She also has a wicked sense of humour and is quick to put people in their place. When Stephanie Crawford tells people that she saw Boo Radley watching her in bed one night, Miss Maudie asks her why she didn't move over and make room for him! She is a strong woman with a mind of her own; she is a Baptist but she refuses to be intimidated by extreme Baptists who think that 'anything that's pleasure is a sin'. She loves annoying the foot-washing Baptists by quoting scripture back at them when they shout abuse at her.

Miss Maudie represents the more positive aspects of Christianity by being charitable and non-judgemental.

Miss Stephanie Crawford

Miss Stephanie, a 'neighborhood scold', is well known in the neighbourhood as a gossip and a busybody. She is a figure of comedy to some extent, because her imagination runs wild and she enjoys a sensational story as much as the children. She has convinced herself and the town that she has seen Boo Radley staring into her bedroom window at night. Miss Maudie is quick to dismiss her tales as nonsense. However, Miss Stephanie is also a good neighbour and welcomes Miss Maudie into her home when Miss Maudie's house is destroyed by fire.

Miss Rachel Haverford

Miss Rachel is Dill's aunt and she takes Dill in every summer. She is one of many relations who take turns at raising Dill.

Mrs Dubose

Mrs Henry Lafayette Dubose is a sick, elderly neighbour who is rumoured to carry a pistol under her shawls and wraps. Jem and Scout fear and hate her. After she passes away, they learn that they had misjudged the woman. Her fits of abuse were due to her drug addiction which she was determined to conquer before she died. In Atticus's view, she was brave and heroic.

Mrs Merriweather

Despite her jolly name, Mrs Merriweather is a very unpleasant character. She is known publicly as the 'most devout lady in Maycomb' but she exemplifies religious hypocrisy. Her role in the novel highlights the more negative aspects of religion and its impact on people's lives.

Dill (Charles Baker Harris)

Dill, the children's summertime companion, is a wonderful addition to the novel. He is adventurous, imaginative and full of life. He is a little bit wild and daring, as a result of having been neglected by his parents. It is said that he is passed around from relation to relation. He is more streetwise than Jem and Scout, knowing about things like strip poker and gambling.

Dill's wild imagination and curiosity are very important to the narrative – it was his idea to make Boo come out. He makes up elaborate fantasies about his wonderful new father, but the reader and most of Maycomb can see that the reality is quite sad. Scout is thrilled when he runs away and turns up in Maycomb, but when he explains how lonely and unloved he felt, the reader can sense great sadness in his life. There is a sensitivity and compassion to Dill which is very appealing. He breaks down in court and has to be taken outside when he sees Tom Robinson being cross-examined. He is disturbed by the 'simple hell' that white people can give to black people.

Based on the real-life author Truman Capote, who was Harper Lee's lifelong friend, it is not surprising that the imaginative Dill grew up to be a world-famous writer.

Bob Ewell

The polar opposite of Atticus, Bob Ewell is the worst father imaginable. He is regarded as 'trash', he never works and he spends his welfare money on drink. His wife is dead and his eldest daughter, Mayella, is left to raise the other children in filth and poverty. His children are extremely neglected and malnourished, and they do not go to school.

Bob Ewell is violent man, a racist and a bully – he beats his daughter when he sees her kissing a black man. In court, he shows himself to be ignorant, rude and vulgar. After the trial, he intimidates Tom Robinson's wife, Helen, following her home and muttering obscene language behind her. Nobody realises how dangerous he is until the end of the novel when he actually tries to kill Jem and Scout. He is the only true villain in the novel, and there is no hope for his children.

Mayella Ewell

Mayella is Bob Ewell's daughter and she is the person who accuses Tom Robinson of rape. When she is on trial, it is clear to the reader that she is lying and that there is no evidence that Tom raped her or attacked her. The facts of the case make it much more likely that her father beat her up when he saw her making advances on Tom.

However, despite the terrible effect she has on Tom's life, she is portrayed as a victim. Atticus describes her as a victim 'of cruel poverty', and Scout believes she is 'the loneliest person in the world', even lonelier than Boo Radley. Mayella lives in filth and tries to raise her brothers and sisters. The only beauty in her life is in the geraniums which she keeps in old jars outside her house. She is truly isolated in society: 'white people wouldn't have anything to do with her because she lived among pigs; Negroes wouldn't have anything to do with her because she was white.' There is also a suggestion during Tom's testimony that her father has sexually abused her in the past.

Mayella's behaviour was considered shameful because it was unthinkable in the American South in the 1930s for any white woman to be attracted to a 'Negro'. White people saw black men as a huge threat to white women, and white women – certainly southern ladies – were meant to be repulsed by black men. The white people of Maycomb simply could not imagine it any other way. When Mayella tried to seduce Tom, she broke 'a time-honoured code' of behaviour, but her extreme loneliness explains why she would do the unthinkable and turn to Tom Robinson for affection.

Tom Robinson

Tom Robinson is a black man who has been accused of raping a white woman, and Atticus is defending him. Tom's character is not explored in great detail – the issues that surround his trial are more important. However, Calpurnia tells

Atticus he has an excellent reputation in his community, he goes to church and is a good father and husband. Reverend Sykes asks for donations for Tom's family at church and Tom's employer stands up in court to tell everyone that Tom has always been a valued employee.

When Tom speaks in court, it is clear that he was helpful and kind towards Mayella. He did odd jobs for her because he pitied her. When she tried to kiss him, he tried not to hurt her feelings and he tried not to be 'rough' with her. He was in a hopeless situation. He could not lay a finger on a white woman, even to push her away, and when Bob Ewell arrived he had no choice but to run. When he tried to escape from prison, it was because he had given up all hope. He is a victim of prejudice and he is the one mockingbird figure who actually is killed. When the guards shoot him down, they shoot him seventeen times.

Aunt Alexandra

Aunt Alexandra is Atticus's sister, but she is very different from Atticus in attitudes and values. Scout says she 'fitted into the world of Maycomb like a hand into a glove'. This is because she is so prejudiced and narrow-minded. She is very conservative and snobbish. When the Finches stay with her at Christmas, her grandson, Cousin Francis, repeats her views that Dill is a 'little runt', Atticus is a 'nigger-lover' and a bad father, and he is disgracing the family name. When she comes to stay with the Finch family before the trial, she says she is there to help Atticus and to exert some 'feminine influence' over Scout, but it is more likely that she wants to take control of his home and stop him from 'ruining' the family name.

Aunt Alexandra takes great pride in the family name and the family 'background'. She is determined to stop Scout being herself – she wants to convert her into 'a lady', and a 'Finch lady' at that. To Aunt Alexandra, being a 'Finch lady' means more than wearing dresses and serving refreshments at tea parties. It means staying away from poor children like Walter Cunningham, whom she regards as 'trash'. She strongly disapproves of Dill too because of his unstable family background. A Finch lady must only mix with 'fine folks', people of 'background'. Aunt Alexandra has a very narrow idea of 'fine folks'. Fine folks, or respectable people, are people with 'background' and their background can be traced back several generations because they have lived on the same patch of land. Aunt Alexandra judges people, not by their character, but by their background. Aunt Alexandra finds fault with most people in Maycomb. For instance, everyone has 'a streak' – a drinking streak or a gambling streak – which they inherited from their family genes. Aunt Alexandra takes ridiculous pride in the Finch family genes.

Aunt Alexandra is not very happy that Atticus is defending Tom Robinson in court. She does not welcome social change. When she comes to stay, she is shocked that the children have visited Calpurnia's church. She even asks Atticus to sack Calpurnia, but Atticus refuses to do this. For most of the novel Scout detests her, but she softens towards her near the end of the novel, and accepts that she may learn something of value from her aunt.

Mr Dolphus Raymond

Mr Dolphus Raymond makes only a brief appearance in the novel (during the trial), but he is a very interesting character who is modern and unconventional (not traditional). Until Scout meets him, she accepts the local opinion that he is a most 'evil' man. After all, he is a white man who has had children with a black woman, he spends all his time with black people and he is believed to be drunk all the time. However, Maycomb turns a blind eye to his lifestyle because he is very rich, he comes from an old family with 'background' and they think he is always drunk, so he can be excused for his behaviour. Scout and Dill are shocked to discover that he has been drinking Coca-Cola all the time, and just lets people think he is a drinker so that they will leave him alone. This 'evil' man is actually a kind man and he hates the way white people mistreat black people. He is also wise and philosophical; he respects children for their sensitivity but warns Dill that adult life will probably change him and make him harder. Scout is amazed that someone would pretend to be 'bad' when everyone else in Maycomb is so obsessed with reputation. Yet again, the people of Maycomb have misjudged somebody, and Scout is learning to be less prejudiced.

Walter Cunningham

Walter is in Scout's class at school and is the child of a poor farmer. His father is one of the many farmers who were badly affected by the Wall Street Crash and the Depression. His family is stuck in the poverty trap. He cannot pass First Grade or receive an education, because he works on the farm instead of attending school. His lack of education will limit his opportunities and confine him to a life of hardship and poverty.

Mr Cunningham

Walter's father is one of the poor farmers affected by the Depression. He is a proud figure who lives in poverty but will not accept charity or welfare money. He will not borrow what he cannot afford to pay back. If he cannot pay for something in money, he will pay in produce from his farm. This is how he pays Atticus for his services as a lawyer.

Mr Cunningham is a complex figure. His darker side is revealed when he arrives with the 'Old Sarum bunch' to lynch Tom. He is clearly prejudiced and seeks a solution in violence and intimidation, yet he changes his mind when Scout chats to him about Walter, and appeals to his better nature. His character illustrates that human beings can be a complex mix of strengths and weaknesses.

Heck Tate

Heck Tate is the sheriff. He is a reasonable man who wants to uphold the law and is generally supportive of Atticus. When Bob Ewell is found dead, Heck is determined to protect Boo Radley. He stands firm on this point and this shows his decency and common sense.

5. Questions for Revision

▶ **CHAPTER ONE**

Why do you think the author mentions slaves early in Chapter One?
What is Atticus's attitude towards Maycomb, according to Scout?
What is your impression of life in Maycomb?
What is Scout's attitude towards Calpurnia?
How did Scout's mother die?
What important details do you learn about the Radley place in this chapter?
Who is Dill?
What is the general attitude in Maycomb towards the Radleys?
Why was Maycomb so shocked by Arthur Radley's 'gang'?
What does Calpurnia say about Mr Radley?
Who came home to take Mr Radley's place when he died?
What does Miss Stephanie say about Boo?
Is Jem's description of Boo 'reasonable', in your opinion? Give reasons for
    your answer.
Why does Jem agree to touch the Radley House?
What is suggested by the last sentence of Chapter One?

▶ **CHAPTER TWO**

How does Scout feel about starting school?
Why does Scout get into trouble with Miss Caroline Fisher?
What details indicate that Walter is poor?

▶ CHAPTER THREE

Why does Jem prevent Scout from fighting Walter?

Why is Calpurnia furious with Scout?

What is Atticus's opinion of Calpurnia?

What do you learn about Burris Ewell's family in this chapter?

How do the children react to Burris's outburst?

What does Calpurnia do to comfort Scout when she comes home?

What crucial advice does Atticus give Scout about understanding people?

What bargain does Atticus make with Scout? What does this tell us about him as a parent?

▶ CHAPTER FOUR

Why does school make Scout feel she is being 'cheated out of something'?

What objects do the children find in the tree?

Name two reasons why Scout wants to 'quit the game'?

▶ CHAPTER FIVE

Why does Scout get annoyed with Dill?

Why does Scout become closer to Miss Maudie?

Describe Miss Maudie's personality.

Why do the 'foot-washing Baptists' condemn Miss Maudie?

Miss Maudie suggests that the bible can be dangerous. What does she mean by this?

Miss Maudie refuses to gossip about Boo Radley, but she gives vital clues about him. What are these clues?

Why do the children get into trouble with Atticus?

▶ CHAPTER SIX

Explain briefly how Jem loses his pants.

Why does Mr Nathan Radley fire his shotgun?

Why is Jem determined to get his pants without telling Atticus?

▶ CHAPTER SEVEN

Why is Jem 'moody and silent' for a week? What has disturbed him?

What special gifts turn up in the tree? What makes these objects so personal?

Why do the children stop receiving gifts from the tree?

▶ CHAPTER EIGHT

Who dies in the winter?

How do Miss Maudie and Atticus react to the children's snowman?

Why does Atticus say 'Looks like all of Maycomb was out tonight, in one way or another'?

Examine Miss Maudie's reaction to her house going up in flames. What does this suggest about her personality?

▶ CHAPTER NINE

What does Cecil Jacobs say about Atticus?

Who is Tom Robinson?

Why is Atticus defending Tom Robinson?

What is Atticus's advice to Scout about fighting? How does Scout handle this advice?

Why is Aunt Alexandra compared to Mount Everest?

How does Cousin Francis echo his grandmother's attitude towards Dill and Atticus?

What advice does Atticus give Uncle Jack about children?

Why is Atticus more worried about Scout than about Jem?

What does Atticus mean by 'Maycomb's usual disease'?

Why does Scout believe Atticus wanted her to hear his conversation with Uncle Jack?

▶ CHAPTER TEN

Why are Scout and Jem embarrassed by their father?

What advice does Atticus give Jem about shooting?

Why does Calpurnia ring the telephone operator?

Why does Heck Tate insist that Atticus shoots the dog?

Describe the atmosphere just before Atticus shoots Tim Johnson.

Why did Atticus give up shooting, despite his talent?

What, in your opinion, is important about this chapter?

▶ CHAPTER ELEVEN

Why are the children afraid of Mrs Dubose?

What gift does Jem buy for Scout?

Why does Scout say that Jem 'simply went mad'?

What is Jem's punishment?

Why does Atticus think that Mrs Dubose was the 'bravest person' he ever knew?

▶ CHAPTER TWELVE

What changes can be seen in Jem?

How is Scout's relationship with Calpurnia changing?

Why does Calpurnia take Scout and Jem to her church?

Why is Calpurnia's church called 'First Purchase'?

How does the congregation react to Jem and Scout when they arrive at First Purchase?

How does Calpurnia appear different to the children when they see her among black people?

What details show that Scout finds First Purchase very different from her own church?

How does the author show that Reverend Sykes is very powerful in his community?

Based on this chapter, what is your impression of the black community in general?

▶ CHAPTER THIRTEEN

Why has Aunt Alexandra come to stay?

What details show that Aunt Alexandra is narrow-minded?

Why do you think Aunt Alexandra fits in so well in Maycomb?

Would you say that Aunt Alexandra's attitude about family 'background' is based on snobbery? Give reasons for your answer.

▶ CHAPTER FOURTEEN

Why do Atticus and Aunt Alexandra have a row which leaves her furious?

Why do Scout and Jem get into a fist fight?

How does Jem 'break the remaining code' of their childhood in this scene?

Why has Dill run away?

▶ CHAPTER FIFTEEN

Why, in your opinion, is the Ku Klux Klan mentioned in this chapter?

Why does Atticus decide to spend the night outside the county jail?

What details create an atmosphere of fear in this chapter?

Why do the Old Sarum bunch tell Atticus that the sheriff won't be available all night?

What do the Old Sarum bunch want from Atticus?

How does Atticus react when he sees his children?

Why do the men decide to leave?

What is important about Mr Underwood's comment after the men leave?

▶ CHAPTER SIXTEEN

What is Atticus's theory about the behaviour of a mob?

According to Atticus, why did Mr Cunningham decide to leave Atticus alone?

Why does Scout say 'It was a gala occasion' when she sees people arriving in town?

What is so unusual about Mr Dolphus Raymond?

Why does Jem say a 'mixed child' is 'real sad'?

▶ CHAPTER SEVENTEEN

Why is Heck Tate questioned on the witness stand?

Does Heck come across as efficient and professional in this scene? Give reasons for your answer.

What two pieces of valuable evidence does Atticus get from Heck Tate?

Name three things that show that the Ewells are a dysfunctional family.

What do the geraniums in jars suggest about Mayella Ewell?

How are the cabins of the 'negroes' different from the Ewells' home?

Based on the answers he gives in court, what kind of father is Bob Ewell?

What vital evidence does Atticus get from Bob Ewell?

▶ CHAPTER EIGHTEEN

Why does Mayella think that Atticus is mocking her?

What kind of home life does Mayella have?

▶ CHAPTER NINETEEN

Which hand is Tom Robinson unable to use?

Why does Scout compare Mayella to a 'mixed child'?

Is Tom Robinson's story more believable than Mayella's, in your opinion? Give reasons for your answer.

When Scout says 'the damage was done', what 'mistake' has Tom Robinson made in the witness stand?

Why, according to Tom Robinson, did he run when Bob Ewell saw him through the window?

Why does Dill have to leave the courtroom?

▶ CHAPTER TWENTY

Why does Scout find Mr Dolphus Raymond 'fascinating'?

According to Mr Raymond, how will Dill change when he gets older?

According to Atticus, what is Mayella's 'offence'?

What is the 'lie as black as Tom Robinson's skin' which Atticus refers to in his closing speech?

▶ CHAPTER TWENTY-ONE

Why is Jem so confident that the jury will not convict Tom Robinson?

Why does Scout mention that none of the jury looked at Tom Robinson?

How do the African-Americans show Atticus their gratitude at the end of the trial?

▶ CHAPTER TWENTY-TWO

What does Atticus mean when he says that the courtroom is 'as much Maycomb as missionary teas'?

Why does Jem compare Maycomb to a 'cocoon'?

Why does Dill want to become a clown? What does this suggest about his attitude towards humanity?

How does Bob Ewell show that he's still angry about the trial?

▶ CHAPTER TWENTY-THREE

What is Atticus's reaction to Bob Ewell's threat?

What will happen if Tom loses his appeal?

According to Atticus, what is 'all adding up'?

Describe Aunt Alexandra's attitude towards the Cunninghams.

Who are the 'four kinds of folks in the world', according to Jem? In what way is this attitude typical of Maycomb?

Is Scout's definition of 'folks' a better one? Explain your answer.

Why does Boo Radley feature in Scout and Jem's discussion of 'folks'?

▶ CHAPTER TWENTY-FOUR

Who are the ladies of the missionary circle and why are they in Scout's house?

Describe Scout's attitude towards the missionary ladies.

Who is Mrs Merriweather referring to when she says 'if we just let them know we forgive 'em, that we've forgotten it, then this whole thing'll blow over'?

Would you agree that Mrs Merriweather is being hypocritical in her attitude towards her fellow Christians? Explain your answer.

Why does Atticus come home to fetch Calpurnia?

▶ CHAPTER TWENTY-FIVE

What is the general reaction of Maycomb to Tom Robinson's death?

What does Mr Ewell say about Tom's death?

▶ CHAPTER TWENTY-SIX

How does Scout feel about Boo Radley? What does this tell us about Scout?

Why, in your opinion, is Hitler mentioned in this chapter?

▶ CHAPTER TWENTY-SEVEN

What 'three things' does Scout comment on at the start of the chapter, and how are they connected?

Describe Scout's costume for the pageant.

▶ CHAPTER TWENTY-EIGHT

Why are the children afraid, on their way home in the dark?

Why does Scout's costume become a problem in this chapter?

Who dies under the tree?

▶ CHAPTER TWENTY-NINE

How does Boo Radley's real appearance differ from Jem's image of him at the start of the novel?

Why does Scout greet Boo like a familiar friend?

▶ CHAPTER THIRTY

- How does Boo's behaviour show that he is not used to company?
- Why do Atticus and Heck have an argument about how Bob Ewell died?
- Why does Heck want to keep Boo's actions a secret? Do you agree with this decision? Explain your answer.
- Why is Boo compared to a mockingbird?
- How do the events of this night relate to the first sentence of the novel?

▶ CHAPTER THIRTY-ONE

- Explain Scout's thoughts as she stands on the Radley porch. Why is this an important moment in the novel?
- How would you describe Scout's mood in the final moments of the novel?

6. Themes and Issues

Prejudice

The word 'prejudice' means pre-judging people, forming an opinion about them before we even know them. *To Kill a Mockingbird* portrays a deeply prejudiced society in which prejudice exists on many levels. While Maycomb is a fictional town, it represents most southern American towns in the 1930s. It is a realistic portrayal of people's attitudes, beliefs and way of life. Harper Lee grew up in a town like Maycomb, so she was very familiar with the attitudes and the racism she describes in her novel.

The strongest form of prejudice in *To Kill a Mockingbird* is racism or racial prejudice. The white people of Maycomb still believed that black people were deeply inferior, that black men were a threat to white women and that black and white people should live separately in society. The novel exposes racism and racist behaviour as deeply immoral and inhumane. What the jury does to Tom Robinson is appalling, yet Lee shows us that a racist community found this perfectly acceptable. Most white people found it entertaining, a 'gala occasion'. (When Harper Lee was a child, nine African-American men in Scottsboro, Alabama, were falsely accused and convicted of raping two white women. It was later proved that the women had not been raped.)

Lee shows us another form of prejudice – one based on social class. Because of the Depression, most people have no money, but snobs continue to be snobs because they have their family name. This kind of prejudice is represented by Aunt Alexandra. 'Fine folks' and educated white people don't mix with poor farmers, who are regarded as 'trash'; girls should not play with boys; the Ewells are even worse than the poor farmers because they live on relief cheques (welfare money). They live outside society, socially and geographically, while people like Aunt Alexandra pretend they don't exist.

The people who suffer most because of prejudice are: Tom Robinson; the African-American community; Boo Radley; poor people such as the Cunninghams; and Mayella Ewell. The Finch family also suffers because Atticus takes a stand against racism.

Religious Hypocrisy

While Lee does not attack religion in itself, she shows us the very negative effects of religion when it is in the wrong hands. Many people in Maycomb claim to be Christians but they are unchristian in their behaviour and attitudes. This makes them hypocrites, and Lee shows us how hypocrites act and think.

The worst hypocrites in the novel are the foot-washing Baptists and the missionary circle. The foot-washing Baptists are stern people who believe that any kind of pleasure is a sin. They accuse Miss Maudie of being a sinner because she enjoys her garden too much, yet if they were truly Christian they would not judge somebody else. Miss Maudie is far more Christian than they are – she is kind, charitable and she believes in equality. She does not judge people like Boo Radley or tell lies about him. Her love of nature shows her appreciation of God's work. In contrast, Mr Radley is a foot-washing Baptist and he is shown to be a cruel father who destroys his son's spirit.

Mrs Merriweather and the ladies of the missionary circle are appalling hypocrites. They meet as a Christian group yet they are uncharitable and arrogant. They have no sympathy for Tom Robinson or his family. They don't even think that their black servants have the right to be in a bad mood after the trial!

Mrs Merriweather regards herself as an expert on the natives in Mruna (where the missionaries work) and she clearly sees them as savages. This goes against everything that Christianity stands for, as the bible teaches that all humans have been created by one God, and all people are equal as children of God. Mrs Merriweather ignores this part of Christianity but has the arrogance to preach to others about Christianity. Mrs Merriweather thinks that northerners are hypocrites because they pretend to believe in racial equality, whereas the southerners are honest people who are openly racist! Mrs Merriweather's name suggests a pleasant, jolly person but she represents the worst in religious hypocrisy.

Growing Up/Coming of Age

To Kill a Mockingbird portrays the joys and the disappointments of growing up. For lucky, privileged white children it can be a time of innocence, wonder, imagination and adventure. Yet for neglected children like Dill, it can be a lonely and unsettling time. For poor children, like Walter Cunningham, it means hard work and very little education. We never see black children in the novel, but we can be sure that they worked in the fields and received little education. For the Ewell children, it means hunger, abuse, isolation and absolutely no hope of a better life.

The novel suggests that growing up threatens precious qualities such as innocence and honesty, and that these may be replaced by prejudice and cynicism. Thus the innocent, non-judging nature of the child is also a mockingbird; it is a beautiful thing but it is endangered. There is also the risk that children may become more cruel and uncaring when they grow up. Mr Dolphus Raymond expresses this view when he says that only children cry when people are cruel to others.

Lee shows us that it is almost impossible to grow up in the South without catching 'Maycomb's usual disease' of racism. Scout often says words like 'nigger-talk' or 'he's just a nigger', because she has grown up listening to this kind of language in Maycomb. Most white children in Maycomb are racist and will grow up to be just like their parents – Cecil Jacobs and Cousin Francis are examples. Dill is not bigoted, and he cries for Tom Robinson, but Dill is also a victim of prejudice and something of an outsider in Maycomb.

After the trial, the children are disillusioned with humanity, and they struggle to understand 'folks'. However, it is uplifting that Scout and Jem see the worst of humanity but, with the right guidance, they still become better people.

The Mockingbird Symbol

The mockingbird serves as a deeply meaningful symbol throughout the novel. It stands for innocence, especially innocence that is threatened or persecuted. Miss Maudie tells the children that mockingbirds 'don't do one thing but sing their hearts out for us. That's why it's a sin to kill a mockingbird'. By associating the mockingbird with beautiful song, we are shown that the mockingbird brings beauty into our lives and we should cherish it for this.

Several characters serve to remind us of the mockingbird – the most obvious being Tom Robinson and Boo Radley. Both men have shown only kindness to others and it would be a sin to hurt them, yet both are persecuted by society. Jem, Scout and Dill constantly remind us of the mockingbird, as their innocence is under attack by the ignorance and racism which surrounds them. When Scout speaks to Mr Cunningham and the Old Sarum bunch outside the county jail, her innocence reaches the men's conscience and stops them in their tracks – Scout's voice is like the song of the mockingbird and it stops the men from harming another mockingbird. Mayella Ewell is not an obvious mockingbird figure, but she is a victim of a terrible upbringing, social prejudice and isolation. Like Boo, she is an outcast. She tries to create some beauty by keeping geraniums in old jars. Her testimony in court shows her to be a fragile, lonely and abused young girl.

The Importance of Role Models

As the novel is narrated by a child, we see how children are greatly influenced by adults – parents, relations, neighbours, teachers. Scout spends a lot of time trying to understand adults and their views. Sometimes she picks up attitudes without realising it. For instance, at the start of the novel she believes everything she hears about Boo Radley and later she asks Atticus why he is 'lawin' for niggers' if everyone says it is wrong to do so. When Atticus explains the importance of obeying one's conscience, we see how adults have a huge responsibility towards children as they help to shape their character early in life.

Atticus is clearly the most positive role model in the novel. He is a mentor as well as a father to Jem and Scout. He will not lie to his children, he explains everything patiently and carefully in terms that they understand, and he leads by example. Miss Maudie says he is the same in his house as he is on the public streets; this means his sense of justice is extended to his everyday life. By being a positive role model who practises what he preaches, his children become better people and they do not catch 'Maycomb's usual disease', racism.

Miss Maudie and Calpurnia are also role models for the children. Like Atticus, Miss Maudie is wise and acts as a mentor to the children. She defends the truth and is a living example of the true meaning of Christianity. Calpurnia is an important role model for Scout; she is a strong, intelligent, hard-working woman who frequently reminds Scout of her manners. When Walter Cunningham comes for dinner, it is Calpurnia who teaches Scout about courtesy and hospitality. Because of Calpurnia's importance in the household and Atticus's high regard for her as a 'faithful member of this family', the children take it for granted that a black adult must be respected and valued as much as any white adult.

Conversely, when we look at Bob Ewell, we see what happens when children lack a role model or only have the worst kind of role model. The first Ewell we see in the novel is Burris Ewell, who turns up on Scout's first day at school. He is aggressive, threatening and abusive. Like all the Ewell children, he will appear on the first day of school every year and then disappear. The authorities have given up on his family. Nobody in Maycomb is even sure how many Ewell children there actually are, and they are generally regarded as 'trash' or 'pigs'. Mayella's only contribution is the destructive and devastating effect she has on Tom Robinson's life and family.

Boo Radley is also the victim of a cruel father. Unlike Bob Ewell, Mr Radley controlled his son's life and broke his spirit, turning him into a 'ghost' of his former self.

Other adults in the novel have a negative effect as role models. Most children insult Jem and Scout because they have listened to their parents' bigoted attitudes. Cousin Francis simply repeats Aunt Alexandra's views about Atticus disgracing the family. Dill survives his broken family because his relations take it in turns to care for him. Without Aunt Rachel and some kindness from Atticus, Dill would probably be living on the streets.

In *To Kill a Mockingbird*, great emphasis is placed on the role of fathers – good fathers, bad fathers, absent fathers – who can have a powerful effect on their children and ultimately on society. However, the novel also reminds us that all adults are role models for children and should take this responsibility very seriously.

7. Examination Guidelines

▶ At Higher Level, you will be questioned on a novel you have studied as part of the Fiction Section in Paper Two.

- Each paper is worth 180 marks and your essay on the novel is worth 30 marks.
- There will be two essay questions on the novel and you will only have to do one.
- You will have about 25 minutes to write your answer.

The exam question will not refer to *To Kill a Mockingbird*; you will be asked to write about 'a novel you have studied'. You may want to write about a novel you have read yourself, but it is usually a better idea to answer on the novel you have studied in class with your teacher. This is because you will have studied the novel in detail, and prepared for the exam by writing about characters and themes, and by practising exam questions on this novel. This level of preparation will be very helpful to you in the exam.

▶ Always take a few minutes to plan your essay. Your plan can be a spider diagram or you can just jot down key words for the points you are going to cover in your essay. There's no need to write full sentences in the plan. Try to organise the points into some kind of order after you have written them down. For example, you could write '1' beside your first point, '2' beside the second and so on. Don't worry about neatness in the plan: it is just rough work.

▶ You must organise your work into paragraphs. If you find it difficult to write in paragraphs, your essay plan is essential. Follow the numbered points in your plan and these can be shaped into paragraphs.

▶ Be careful with spellings. Identify words that you find difficult and learn the correct spelling now. Look over words that have been corrected in homework or schoolwork. At the very least, you should be able to spell the names of characters and themes in the novel (e.g. Atticus, Mayella, prejudice).

▶ Start your question by introducing the novel, the author and the setting e.g. 'I have studied *To Kill a Mockingbird* by Harper Lee. This American novel is set in the fictional town of Maycomb in 1930s Alabama.'

▶ Use speech marks (quotation marks) for the title of the novel and for any words taken directly from the novel.

▶ Refer to the words in the question in your introduction.

▶ You should know about the novel's setting, plot, characters and themes, and you should be able to analyse or discuss some key scenes in detail.

▶ You need to know the plot very well in order to write a good answer in the exam, but do not just summarise (or relate) the plot in your answer. You should be able to write about key characters, themes or events in the novel, giving your opinion on them and using examples from the novel to support your points.

▶ A few well-chosen quotations will impress the examiner, but referring to specific details from the story will also work in your favour. Only use quotations if they help you to emphasise a particular point.

▶ Use previous exam papers to practise writing answers on the novel. The more you practise, the easier it will be on the day of the exam. You'll also find that important points will come quickly to you in the exam if you have had plenty of practice at writing about these points before. This will be very useful when you are working against the clock in the exam.

▶ Keep an eye on the time. It is a good idea to write the time at which you started your answer at the top of the page. For example, if you start your answer on the novel at 10.15, you know you should be finishing at about 10.40.

▶ Do not end your answer abruptly. Think about your conclusion (last paragraph) before you write the essay. The conclusion should link with the words in the question itself and should sum up your points. When you read over a conclusion it should sound like an ending to an essay.

8. How to Write an Essay

How to Write an Opening Paragraph

You must name the novel and the author in your opening paragraph. You should make a brief comment on the plot and the setting.

Underline the key (most important) words in the question. Your opening paragraph should contain these key words, as you will be dealing with these in your essay.

You do not need to tell or summarise the story from the beginning – in the course of your essay, your examples and quotations from the novel will show the examiner that you already know the story very well.

Example One

2008

> **From a novel or short story you have studied, choose some features of the writer's style which you found interesting. Explain your choices with reference to your chosen text.**
>
> **(30 marks)**

Opening Paragraph:

I have studied 'To Kill a Mockingbird', by Harper Lee. This novel is set in a small American town in the 1930s and is narrated by Scout Finch, a young tomboy who lives with her father and older brother. This novel is about Scout's childhood and the trial of an African-American man accused of raping a white woman. I found many features of the writer's style interesting, but the one which interested me most was the author's ability to create suspense and tension at very dramatic moments in the novel.

Example Two

2006

> **From a novel or short story you have studied, choose a character you would either like to be or not like to be.**
> **Explain your choice of character with reference to your chosen text.**
> **(30 marks)**

Opening Paragraph:

I have studied 'To Kill a Mockingbird', by Harper Lee. This novel is set in the fictional town of Maycomb, Alabama, during the Great Depression of the 1930s. A character I would not like to be is Mayella Ewell, a young woman who falsely accuses a black man of rape. Mayella lives in filth and poverty and the novel's narrator, Scout Finch, describes her as 'the loneliest person in the world'.

How to Develop and Support a Point

Students often make a brief point or statement without developing it or supporting it with an example from the text. When you make a point in English, you should aim to convince your reader of this point. You can do this by giving examples from the text which prove or illustrate your point. You could mention your chosen example or you could give an exact quotation from the text. When you do this, you are using 'textual support'. Consider the examples below.

Example One

In Part One of the novel, Scout and Jem underestimate their father, Atticus. Before he shoots the mad dog, they think he is 'feeble' and they complain that 'Our father didn't do anything'. They don't fully appreciate or understand his work and would prefer it if he drove a truck or worked in a shop. They are also embarrassed because they think he is not talented. When Miss Maudie tells them that he can play the jew's harp, Scout is even more ashamed of her father.

    Point = Scout and Jem underestimate Atticus.

    Quotation = 'Our father didn't do anything.'

    Development and Examples = They don't fully appreciate or understand his work and would prefer it if he drove a truck or worked in a shop. They are also embarrassed because they think he is not talented. When Miss Maudie tells them that he can play the jew's harp, Scout is even more ashamed of her father.

Example Two

When Atticus shoots the mad dog, Scout and Jem realise that they misjudged their father and they see him in a whole new light. They thought he was feeble and lacked accomplishments, but in fact he was the 'deadest shot in Maycomb'. They learn not to be fooled by appearances.

Point = When Atticus shoots the mad dog, Scout and Jem realise that they misjudged their father and they see him in a whole new light.

Quotation = 'deadest shot in Maycomb'.

Development = They thought he was feeble and lacked accomplishments, but in fact he was the 'deadest shot in Maycomb'. They learn not to be fooled by appearances.

Example Three

Calpurnia is like a strict parent to Scout. When Walter Cunningham comes to visit, Scout unintentionally insults him and Calpurnia is furious with her. We see here that Calpurnia is much more than just a maid – she teaches Scout manners and sensitivity towards others.

Point = Calpurnia is like a strict parent to Scout.

Development and Example = When Walter Cunningham comes to visit, Scout unintentionally insults him and Calpurnia is furious with her. We see here that Calpurnia is much more than just a maid – she teaches Scout manners and sensitivity towards others.

Over to You

Write out the following statements, support each one with a quotation or example from the text, and develop your point:

- Atticus was not a typical parent of the 1930s.
- Boo Radley is a victim of gossip and lies.
- Scout felt great pity for Mayella Ewell in court.
- Lee shows how Christians are often hypocritical and unchristian in their behaviour and attitudes.
- Mr Dolphus Raymond is a very interesting character.

How to Write a Conclusion

The conclusion is the final paragraph of your essay; it is your 'last word'. Many students find this the most difficult part of the question as they've made their points and they feel they have nothing left to say. However, if you don't write a concluding paragraph, your essay will end abruptly and it will be incomplete. When you come to the final paragraph, look back at the key words in the question and at your opening paragraph. You should briefly sum up the points you made in your essay, referring once more to the key words in the question.

Never start a new point or argument in your conclusion.

Study the examples below.

2008 Higher Level Question 2

Sample Conclusion:

In conclusion, the above scenes from 'To Kill a Mockingbird' were dramatic and exciting with lots of suspense and atmosphere. They demonstrate a style of writing which I found interesting and compelling.

2007 Higher Level Question 2

From a novel or short story you have read describe a character that impressed you and explain why this character did so.

Sample Conclusion:

In conclusion, I was very impressed by Atticus because he was an individual who stood for equality and justice. He was surrounded by hypocrites and racists, yet he tried not to judge these people. He was an excellent example to his children and he made a real difference in people's lives.

2006 Higher Level Question 2

Sample Conclusion:

By the time Mayella is finished in court, she emerges as a victim of poverty, ignorance, social isolation and a dysfunctional family. Even though the jury convicts Tom, no one truly believes her or her father. The trial is a humiliating experience for her and all her dark secrets become public. After the trial, her life will go on but it will not improve; if anything, her shame and isolation are made worse by the trial. Mayella also has to live with her conscience, knowing that she is ultimately responsible for Tom Robinson's death. For all of the above reasons, I would not like to be Mayella Ewell.

9. Useful Phrases

You know by now that it is not enough to summarise or re-tell the whole plot of *To Kill a Mockingbird*. You want to show the examiner that you have studied the novel in detail, that you have thought about its characters, themes and issues, and that you have formed opinions on them. You should know the novel so well that you can even support your opinions with quotations and references to scenes in the novel.

If you find yourself 'stuck for words' sometimes, the following phrases may help you to analyse – not summarise – the novel and to express your opinion:

I enjoyed the scene where...

This scene was very important because...

I liked the way this scene was written because...

This character played an important role in the novel because...

I learned a lot from this scene as...

I enjoyed reading about...

The dialogue was...

.../...

The detailed descriptions brought X to life . . .

This was a realistic description . . .

It was difficult to imagine . . .

The language was . . .

The relationship between X and Y was very positive/negative/
interesting/unusual.

I was impressed/not impressed/disappointed/moved by . . .

I found the ending satisfying/moving/disappointing/believable/
unrealistic/dramatic . . .

It was very entertaining/gripping/compelling when . . .

I found X disturbing.

The issue that interested me most in this novel was . . .

10. Students' FAQs — Frequently Asked Questions

Q: 'How long should my essay on the novel be?'

A: There is no set 'length' for an essay because every student is different and every answer is different too. On average, answers on the novel range in length from one and a half to two and a half pages. If you write less than this, you might not answer in enough detail; if you write more you may run out of time. Bear in mind that some students write faster than others and the size of people's handwriting varies, so it is impossible to say precisely how long an essay 'should' be.

Q: 'Should my essay be just like the sample answers in this book?'

A: No. Your essay should reflect your personal response to the novel. The purpose of the sample answers in this book is to show you how you could structure your essay, how you might express opinions, and how to support these opinions. They also show you how to develop points and expand on them.

Q: 'Some people learn essays off by heart for the exam. Is this a good idea?'

A: No. Every year, the exam questions are worded differently, so it is unlikely that you will be able to match a memorised essay to the question. The examiner wants to test – and reward – your personal response, your thinking and writing skills; not your ability to copy someone else's ideas. An examiner will quickly sense that you are not writing in your own 'voice'. Memorising essays is also a limited and unnecessary form of learning. If you want to memorise something, learn some quotations! The Chief Examiner's report on the Junior Certificate exams of 2006 warns students against 'the practice of drilling prepared, rote answers'.

Q: 'How can I show the examiner everything I've learnt in 25 minutes?'

A: You can't. A lot of time will be spent in the classroom on the novel, and hopefully you will invest a lot of time in studying it too, but it is impossible to show an examiner how much you have gained from your work on the novel. Your answer is rather like a snapshot photo which gives the examiner a brief impression of your effort and ability as a student.

Q: 'What is the difference between a quotation and a reference?'

A: When you write down the exact words spoken by a character, and you place them in speech (quotation) marks, you are using a quotation. 'Tom was a dead man the minute Mayella Ewell opened her mouth and screamed' is a quotation. When you refer to, or mention, something from the novel, you are using a reference: for example, if you say, 'Atticus encouraged Scout to use her intelligence, instead of physically fighting all the time', you are making a reference to the novel.'

Q: 'How many quotations should I use in my essay?'

A: There is no set number of quotations. Some people aim for one in every paragraph, but this is not essential. If you find it difficult to remember them, try learning very short quotations, e.g. Scout thought Boo Radley was a 'malevolent phantom'.

Q: 'What are the most important scenes or chapters?'

A: Every moment counts in *To Kill a Mockingbird* because it is so well written, but if you want to pay close attention to some scenes you could focus on:

- all interactions with Boo Radley
- Atticus shooting the mad dog
- Jem and Mrs Dubose
- visiting Calpurnia's church
- the Old Sarum bunch
- Tom Robinson's trial
- meeting Mr Dolphus Raymond
- Boo Radley saving the children's lives.

Q: 'Do I need to write about the historical background?'

A: This is not necessary, but understanding the historical background will give you a much better understanding of the novel. It helps if you know a little about slavery, the southern states of the USA and the Depression.

11. Past Examination Questions and Sample Answers

2008 Higher Level

Select a novel or short story you have studied which deals with a loving relationship or an unloving relationship.

(a) Describe how this relationship develops.   (15 marks)

(b) Choose one of the characters in this relationship and imagine yourself in his/her situation. How do you see the other character in the relationship? Write your ideas based on evidence from the text.   (15 marks)

Approaching the Question

▶ For this answer, you could describe Scout's loving relationship with Atticus or Jem or Calpurnia, or Jem's loving relationship with Atticus, or you could write about Bob Ewell's unloving relationship with his children. You should write about how this relationship grows or develops over the course of the novel.

▶ For part (b), you can write from the point of view of your chosen character. 'Based on evidence from the text' means that you should use details from the story as examples to support or back up what you say about the characters in question.

Sample Answer

(a)

I have studied 'To Kill a Mockingbird', by Harper Lee. This novel is set in a small southern town in the United States in the 1930s and is narrated by a young girl called Scout Finch who lives with her father, Atticus, and her brother, Jem. Atticus is a lawyer and his wife is dead, so Scout and Jem are raised by their black maid, Calpurnia. A loving relationship develops between Scout and Calpurnia.

At first, this relationship does not appear to be loving. As a small child, Scout is always in trouble and Calpurnia rules with a firm hand. 'Our battles were epic and one-sided. Calpurnia always won, mainly because Atticus always took her side.' Scout resents Calpurnia's authority and feels that Calpurnia never fights with Jem, her brother. However, Atticus reminds Scout that this may be because Jem does not give Cal as much trouble as Scout does.

Calpurnia is like a strict parent to Scout. When Walter Cunningham comes to visit, Scout unintentionally insults him and Calpurnia is furious with her. We see here that Calpurnia is much more than just a maid – she teaches Scout manners and sensitivity towards others. Atticus sees Calpurnia as a 'faithful member' of the family; he trusts Calpurnia to raise his children as well as run his household.

Scout's relationship with Calpurnia improves over time. Scout hates being a girl, as the boys (Jem and Dill) often exclude her from their games. In her loneliness, she often turns to Calpurnia for company. The reader can see that Calpurnia is very fond of Scout, as she misses her when she starts school. Calpurnia's love of Scout is also evident in the way that she never criticises Scout for being a tomboy, playing with boys or wearing overalls. She gives Scout the freedom to be herself and Scout comes to admire her for the work she does. She also sees that she can learn a lot from Calpurnia about being 'a lady'.

A turning point in their relationship comes when Scout and Jem visit Calpurnia's church, First Purchase, as Scout sees for the first time that Calpurnia has a completely different life outside the Finch household. Cal speaks with a different accent among her own community and her grammar is careless; Scout calls it 'nigger talk', but it is the colloquial language used by African-Americans in Alabama. When Scout questions Cal about this, she explains that she does not want to intimidate people or stand out, by sounding more educated than others. Yet when she is with the Finches, she speaks as they do in order to fit in. Scout is very impressed that Cal has 'command of two languages' but she also wonders at her 'modest double life'. She asks Calpurnia many questions about her church and her community, and Calpurnia answers all of them. These questions and answers show that they can communicate openly and freely about anything. It is a warm and trusting relationship.

Later in the novel, when Aunt Alexandra tries to get Atticus to dismiss Calpurnia, Scout is horrified. Their relationship has come a long way and Scout has come to love and value Calpurnia for the vital role she plays in her life.

(b)

I have chosen to imagine that I am Scout and I will write about Calpurnia from her point of view.

'Calpurnia has been in my life for as long as I can remember. My mother died when I was two, so I don't remember her. I've been really lucky to have Calpurnia here to take her place. Of course, I didn't always appreciate her! When I was little I thought she was always picking on me, but that's because I was such a handful. I was my daddy's little pet and I used to be really hurt when he took Calpurnia's side against me, but he trusted her to raise me and teach me right from wrong. He believed she had really good "radar". In other words, he trusted her judgement and her instinct.

'Calpurnia was strict but she was very fair. She never stopped me from playing with Jem and Dill, even though most of the neighbours thought I was a disgrace. She also allowed me to wear overalls, which scandalised the neighbours. The only time she made me wear a dress was when we went to her church. The night before, she put so much starch in my dress that it came up like a tent! She took great pride in us that day and she really regarded us as her own children. She also stood up for us when a woman called Lula tried to have us thrown out of church. I was stunned at Calpurnia's nerve and how she spoke to Lula: "Stop right there, nigger". I saw a whole new side to Cal that day – she led a double life! She practically spoke two languages.

'Calpurnia knew how to act in an emergency. When a mad dog with rabies approached our street, Calpurnia warned the whole town and sent for Atticus and the sheriff. She managed to get everyone in off the streets in seconds. She always seemed to know how to act in a crisis. She was the same when we got the awful news that Tom Robinson was dead. We had a few moments to react and then Cal went with Atticus to tell Tom's wife, Helen.

Calpurnia really was a faithful member of our family and she gave me all the love and guidance that my mother would have given me if she hadn't died when I was two.'

2008 Higher Level

From a novel or short story you have studied, choose some features of the writer's style which you found interesting. Explain your choices with reference to your chosen text.

(30 marks)

Approaching the Question

▶   You could discuss several features of a writer's style, for example:
- first-person narrative
- descriptive skill
- story-telling skill
- imagery and symbolism
- characterisation.

Sample Answer

I have studied 'To Kill a Mockingbird', by Harper Lee. This novel is set in a small American town in the 1930s and is narrated by Scout Finch, a young tomboy who lives with her father and older brother. This novel is about Scout's childhood and the trial of an African-American man accused of raping a white woman. I found many features of the writer's style interesting, but the one which interested me most was the author's ability to create suspense and tension at very dramatic moments in the novel.

There are many dramatic scenes in the novel which show the author's skilful use of suspense, and one of these scenes takes place when Scout's father, Atticus, is forced to save the town from a rabid dog. The author creates an atmosphere of fear and tension by describing the event in great detail. First, the children spot the dog coming towards them and they can tell something is wrong because he is 'lopsided'. When Calpurnia sees him, she panics:

'Calpurnia stared, then grabbed us by the shoulders and ran us home.'

Calpurnia then rings Atticus at work, rings the operator, Eula May, and warns all the neighbours to stay inside. She even runs onto the Radley porch to warn them. It is unheard of for a black woman to do this; she is supposed to use the back door, but there is no time. The whole neighbourhood gets involved and the sheriff arrives with Atticus, who is carrying a rifle. All these details are a feature of the writer's style and they show the reader that the threat of this dog is very serious.

When Atticus arrives with the sheriff, the tension increases as we learn that Atticus hasn't shot a gun in thirty years. Worse still, his glasses fall to the ground and break. The children are terrified as they have no idea that their father is able to shoot a gun. Lee's description of atmosphere is excellent: 'Nothing is more deadly than a deserted, waiting street.' It sounds like a scene from a western with a showdown between two cowboys!

Scout's thoughts are shared with the reader and they add to the drama: 'He walked quickly, but I thought he moved like an underwater swimmer; time had slowed to a nauseating crawl.' When Atticus shoots the dog, he saves the day and the children realise that their father is a true hero, 'the deadest shot in Maycomb'.

Another example of Harper Lee's style can be seen when Atticus is threatened by the Old Sarum bunch outside the town jail. This scene takes place the night before Tom Robinson's trial. The chapter opens with talk of the Ku Klux Klan and this creates tension and an awareness of the danger and violence surrounding the trial. When Atticus leaves the house that night, the children are afraid for him so they sneak out and follow him to the jail. Once more, the author uses details to create a fearful, tense atmosphere. The whole square is deserted, so Atticus is alone when the men from Old Sarum approach him. Their approach is eerie and threatening: 'Shadows became substance as light revealed solid shapes moving towards the jail door.' To make matters worse, the men tell Atticus that the sheriff will be away in the woods all night, so Atticus is totally deserted. Scout's thoughts and fears are shared with the reader once again and they show how frightening this situation is: 'I began to feel sweat gathering at the edges of my hair; I could stand anything but a bunch of people looking at me.'

The tension is broken when Scout rushes forward and starts chatting to Mr Cunningham, causing the men to turn around and leave. This scene is an excellent example of the author's style of writing.

The most dangerous scene in the novel takes place when the children are almost murdered by Bob Ewell. In this scene, the children are returning from a Hallowe'en pageant in utter darkness. They sense that someone is following them because they hear footsteps behind them but they cannot see a thing. When they stop, the footsteps stop. They also hear a rustling sound but they know it is not the wind: 'what I thought were trees rustling was the soft swish of cotton on cotton, wheek, wheek, with every step'. They have no idea who is following them, but there is definitely a presence behind them and the children are beginning to panic. Suddenly they are attacked in the dark and Scout is trapped in her costume which is made of chicken wire. Scout describes the costume as a 'wire prison' as she is restricted by it. A stranger grabs her in the dark and 'slowly [squeezes] the breath out of [her]'. Luckily Boo Radley comes to the rescue, saving the children's lives. This scene is yet another example of a dramatic moment, full of suspense and tension.

In conclusion, the above scenes from 'To Kill a Mockingbird' were dramatic and exciting with lots of suspense and atmosphere. They demonstrate a style of writing which I found interesting and compelling.

2007 Higher Level

Select a novel or short story you have studied which you would recommend to your own age group and explain why you would recommend it.

(30 marks)

Approaching the Question

▷   In answering this question, you should focus on why this novel would appeal to people of your age. You should refer to aspects of the novel that you enjoyed, because these elements may appeal to other young people too.

Extract from Junior Certificate Marking Scheme, 2007:

Any valid reasons acceptable, for example:

- dramatic, exciting story
- interesting, appealing characters
- engaging themes and emotions
- imaginative setting
- good lesson to be learned from story
- etc.

Sample Answer

I would strongly recommend the novel 'To Kill a Mockingbird', by Harper Lee, to my own age group. This novel was written in the late 1950s during the Civil Rights Movement in the United States and it was set in the 1930s, but it can still be enjoyed by young people today for many reasons.

One of the reasons that this novel would appeal to young people today is that it tells a really gripping and exciting story. The novel is narrated by a young tomboy, Jean Louise Finch (Scout), who describes a sleepy, quiet southern town called Maycomb where nothing much seems to happen. Scout grows up there with her brother, Jem, and her best friend, Dill. For these children, Maycomb could have been a very boring place, but thanks to the children's imagination and curiosity they have no shortage of excitement and adventure. The source of excitement and fear is Boo Radley, a local recluse who has not left his house for years. The children are fascinated and terrified by this man and they dream of 'making Boo Radley come out'. Boo fascinates the children because they have heard so many stories about him. They believe he is a 'malevolent phantom' responsible for all bad things that happen in the neighbourhood: 'When people's azaleas froze in a cold snap, it was because he had breathed on them. Any stealthy crimes committed in Maycomb were his work.' No child will eat the pecans that fall from the Radleys' trees and nobody will retrieve a ball that lands in their garden: 'Radley pecans would kill you. A baseball hit into the Radley yard was a lost ball and no questions asked.'

The mystery of Boo Radley makes for great reading as it lends the book an element of adventure and mystery which is really appealing to young people. It is also appealing to young people because it treats the mystery of Boo in an intelligent way – there are reasons why Boo is a 'ghost', as well as a victim of gossip, superstition and prejudice. These reasons are revealed in the course of the novel, and they add to its enjoyment.

I would also recommend this novel to my age group because the themes of the novel are still relevant today – prejudice, social isolation, racism, injustice, growing up. These themes remain relevant because they are universal – they affect all people in all places.

'To Kill a Mockingbird' looks at all types of prejudice – racial, social and otherwise. The book's main message comes from Scout's father when he tells her not to judge another person until she has seen things from their point of view, 'until you climb into his skin and walk around in it'. This is a very difficult thing to do. Scout and Jem judge Mrs Dubose, their neighbour, to be 'the meanest woman' alive, yet they discover that she was actually the 'bravest woman' that Atticus ever knew. Scout is certain that Mr Dolphus Raymond is a truly 'evil man', yet when she meets him she learns that this 'evil' man is actually a compassionate man who hates the way white people mistreat black people.

The novel also looks at social isolation. People in Maycomb like to pretend that the Ewell family does not exist. Each year, Maycomb gives them 'Christmas baskets and the back of its hand'. They are regarded as 'trash', even 'pigs'. The authorities have given up on them; nobody is sure how many children are in the family and the truancy officer just makes sure they turn up on the first day of school each year. I enjoyed the way the novel constantly examined the theme of social isolation, because in Ireland today we still isolate many groups and exclude them from everyday life.

The strongest form of discrimination in the novel is racism, 'Maycomb's usual disease'. I learned a lot from the novel's treatment of racism and I think many readers my age would learn from it too, because it is a part of life in Ireland today. The novel shows us the damage and suffering caused by racism. Racism has a terrible effect on the black community in the novel – they are poorly educated, they are victims of discrimination and segregation and they can only ever work as badly paid servants to white people. The Finch family suffers because of racism – Scout and Jem are constantly bullied in school because their father is a 'nigger-lover', while Atticus is threatened by the mob from Old Sarum when they come to lynch Tom Robinson.

The biggest victim of racism is Tom Robinson. Atticus says 'Tom was a dead man the minute Mayella Ewell opened her mouth and screamed.' Tom loses his life to racism and his family loses their father. Like the mockingbird, he is an innocent victim and the way he is treated is a sin. Many young readers are aware of racism but don't really understand how destructive and inhumane it actually is, so I would definitely recommend 'To Kill a Mockingbird' to my own age group because I think it is essential reading on this issue.

Finally, I would recommend this novel to my age group because it is about growing up and we are still growing up! The novel shows how growing up and coming of age can be a difficult time. Sooner or later, we all have to grow up, lose our innocence and face the ugly side of human nature. Like Scout and Jem, young people often find it difficult to accept the world as it is. We live in a world where innocence is quickly lost and it is hard not to become cynical or just give up on humanity. After Tom Robinson's trial, Dill says that when he grows up he will be a clown, but he will be a special type of clown that just laughs back at the human race. I think a lot of young readers will identify with this as there is so much injustice and inequality in the world today that it is easy to just give up on the human race. However, the novel's ending shows us that we don't have to do that. Sometimes good triumphs over evil and sometimes people change their attitudes, even if that happens very slowly.

In conclusion, I would be happy to recommend 'To Kill a Mockingbird' to my own age group, because I am sure they will find it entertaining, memorable and relevant.

2007 Higher Level

From a novel or short story you have read describe a character that impressed you and explain why this character did so.

(30 marks)

Approaching the Question

▶ There are many characters who are impressive in this novel – Atticus, Calpurnia, Boo Radley, Jem, Scout, Miss Maudie – so you have plenty to choose from for this answer. Focus on a character who played an important part in the novel. Don't just describe the character – it is important that you explain why they impressed you. You should give examples of things they said and things they did that impressed you. You can also look at things people say about them. For example, Miss Maudie explains many of Atticus's qualities and this makes him an even more impressive character.

Extract from **Junior Certificate Marking Scheme, 2007:**

Answers should not be simple summary.
The description might focus on:

- the character's actions, attitudes, behaviour, beliefs, personality, etc.

The explanation as to why the character impressed the reader might refer to:

- the character as hero, villain, person of action, feeling, thought, role model, etc.

Sample Answer

I have studied 'To Kill a Mockingbird', by Harper Lee. This novel is set in the fictional town of Maycomb, Alabama during the Great Depression of the 1930s. A character who really impressed me was Atticus Finch, the father of the novel's young narrator, Scout Finch. He impressed me as a parent, a lawyer and as a human being. Atticus was a single parent because his wife died when his children were very small, but he still managed to be an excellent father, despite a demanding job as a lawyer.

As a parent, Atticus was unique and I found this very interesting. He raised his children according to his principles and this often shocked people. For instance, he allowed his daughter, Scout, to play with boys and to wear trousers when no other girls were allowed to do this. He didn't worry about appearances or put pressure on Scout to be a 'lady'. He accepted her as she was, even if the neighbours thought this was disgraceful. He also allowed his children to call him by his first name and he never lied to them, even if they asked him difficult questions. He believed that lies only confused children.

Atticus was strict with his children, yet he never laid a finger on them. This was very progressive for the 1930s, as most parents would have felt entitled to slap or even whip their children for misbehaviour. As a result, the children trust and respect Atticus and they always accept their punishment when they have done wrong. When Atticus punished Jem for destroying Mrs Dubose's camellias, he was teaching Jem respect and tolerance, but he also wanted Jem to learn about 'real courage'. Jem had no idea that Mrs Dubose was a morphine addict and that she was determined to break her addiction before she died, so he and Scout had judged her without knowing all of the facts about her. Jem hated his punishment, but he learned from the experience.

Atticus impressed me because he was so wise. He gave his children excellent advice about life and about the world they lived in. For instance, he told his children 'You never really understand a person until you consider things from his point of view . . . until you climb into his skin and walk around in it.' This advice deals with one of the main themes of the novel – prejudice. This was very relevant to the children because they lived in such a prejudiced, racist society where people constantly judged others without really knowing them. His advice was difficult to follow but it helped his children to think for themselves and to become more understanding of people. Atticus also told his son to "Shoot all the bluejays you want...but remember it's a sin to kill a mockingbird." This advice was not just about hunting. Atticus was trying to teach his children to be more compassionate and humane towards others, especially innocent people who had caused harm to nobody. Thanks to Atticus's guidance and advice, his children became compassionate, non-racist individuals who could think for themselves.

Atticus didn't just give advice and preach to his children; he also led by example. This is evident when he agreed to represent Tom Robinson, a black man wrongly accused of raping a white woman, in court. Atticus knew that his actions would make him very unpopular in Maycomb and probably across all of Alabama, as it was a very high-profile case. He knew he would be ridiculed and threatened by people. People would call him a 'nigger-lover' and his children would be bullied in school, but he refused to back down as he knew he had to obey his conscience. This showed great strength of character and courage. He explained his reasons for representing Tom Robinson to his children, so that they would see how important it is to do the right thing, even when it is the most difficult choice:

'This case, Tom Robinson's case, is something that goes to the essence of a man's conscience – Scout, I couldn't go to church and worship God if I didn't try to help that man.'

This is one of the things I liked most about Atticus and it was another quality which made him stand out from the crowd.

I really admired Atticus's determination and his long-term vision. He knew that Tom hadn't a hope in court – 'Tom was a dead man the minute Mayella Ewell opened her mouth and screamed' – yet he fought tooth and nail for him in court. Atticus did this because he knew that it was still vital to defend the truth and to show society that a black man deserved a fair trial and full legal representation. This sounds very normal today but to white southerners in the 1930s, it was shocking and radical. Atticus knew that the case was an important step in the right direction for human rights and in the fight against 'Maycomb's usual disease', racism. This shows his long-term vision and his determination to change his world.

In conclusion, I was very impressed by Atticus because he was an individual who stood for equality and justice. He was surrounded by hypocrites and racists, yet he tried not to judge these people. He was an excellent example to his children and he made a real difference in people's lives.

2006 Higher Level

Choose a novel OR short story that has a strong sense of place or setting.

(a) Describe this place or setting. (15 marks)
(b) How is this place or setting important in the novel or short story you have chosen? Support your answer with reference to the novel or short story.

(15 marks)

Approaching the Question

▶ Pay attention to the marking scheme. Each part carries equal marks. Pay attention to the wording of part (b). You must show that Maycomb is important in the story, because the things which happened in the story could only happen in a racist, hypocritical and insular environment. Things would have worked out differently for Tom Robinson if he had not lived in the Deep South in a small town which 'grew inward'.

Sample Answer

(a)

The novel I have studied is called 'To Kill a Mockingbird', by Harper Lee. The setting of this novel is the fictional town of Maycomb, Alabama in the American South. While Maycomb is not a real town, it is typical of many small southern towns in the 1930s and it is based on the town of Monroeville where Harper Lee grew up. The novel's narrator, Scout Finch, lives in Maycomb with her brother and father, Jem and Atticus.

In the novel's first chapter, the narrator creates a picture of a sleepy, dull town where very little happens:

> 'Maycomb was an old town, but it was a tired old town when I first knew it . . . People moved slowly then . . . There was no hurry, for there was nowhere to go, nothing to buy and no money to buy it with . . .'

Like every other town in the United States, Maycomb was affected by the Depression, so money was scarce.

Maycomb was an insular town and the narrator tells us that it 'grew inward'. Scout's family is related to practically everyone by marriage. Because Maycomb was so small and because life was so uneventful, neighbours knew everybody else's business. People knew everyone's family history, going back several generations. This meant that people were constantly judged by their family background and it was impossible to escape your family reputation. The community of Maycomb was full of nosey people who liked to gossip about others. For instance, Miss Stephanie Crawford was known as the 'neighbourhood scold'. She was an incurable gossip, just as Scout's Aunt Alexandra was an incurable snob. These characters represent the general small-town mentality.

While everyone was affected by the Depression, Maycomb was still a very unequal town where racism and prejudice were accepted as the norm. Like any southern town at that time, it was a segregated town. Black and white people attended separate schools and churches, and black people did not have the same rights as white people. Most black people worked as servants to white people and very few of them could read or write because they had to leave school early to go out to work. When the children visit First Purchase, an African-American church, they see that there are no bibles or hymn books because most people cannot read them. Calpurnia, their maid, can read and write but she is an exception.

(b)

The setting of Maycomb is very important in the novel, because it affects the community's outlook and how they treat each other. For instance, it was a southern town so this made it a segregated and deeply racist town. Black people would have had more rights and freedom in the northern states. During the court scene, the children talk about Mr Dolphus Raymond, a rich white man who has had children by a black woman. To escape the racism which is typical of Maycomb, he sends some of his children to live in a northern state.

The setting of the novel is also important for the character of Boo Radley. When Boo was young, Maycomb over-reacted to his 'gang' and the police got involved. His friends were sent away to an industrial school and he was severely punished by his father because he had disgraced his family. In a big city, Boo's 'gang' would never have got so much attention and he might have gone on to lead a normal life, instead of becoming a recluse and a social outcast.

The setting of Maycomb is vital in the trial of Tom Robinson. Tom was an African-American man accused of raping a white woman, Mayella Ewell, and Scout's father, Atticus, was his lawyer. In a town like Maycomb, it was impossible for Tom to get a fair trial. Most people in Maycomb didn't even think a black man should be entitled to his day in court and they were shocked that Atticus would agree to represent him. Atticus was even threatened by a mob of farmers, the Old Sarum bunch, who wanted to break into the jail and take Tom Robinson away the night before his trial. No doubt they would have lynched him. This shows that while Maycomb was a sleepy old town, there was the potential for violence when it came to race.

Atticus managed to protect Tom and represent him in court, but he could not keep Maycomb's racism and ignorance out of the courtroom. The white people of Maycomb saw the trial as entertainment and treated it as a 'gala occasion'. During the trial, it is clear that there was not one iota of medical evidence that Tom had raped Mayella Ewell. It was also virtually impossible for him to beat her up, as she had been beaten on the right of her face and he did not have the use of his left hand, due to a disability. Her father, on the other hand, was left-handed. Everyone in Maycomb knew that the Ewells were a disgrace to the county and they could not be trusted to tell the truth. Yet, despite the lack of evidence, the all-white jury of Maycomb declared Tom guilty. The setting made a huge difference to Tom's life because he now faced the death penalty.

In conclusion, the setting of Maycomb was essential to the story because it was a typical southern town in the 1930s where racism, ignorance and prejudice were a part of everyday life. In a different setting, characters like Boo Radley and Tom Robinson might have had very different lives and Scout would have had a very different story to tell.

2006 Higher Level

From a novel or short story you have studied, choose a character you would either like to be or not like to be. Explain your choice of character with reference to your chosen text.

(30 marks)

Approaching the Question

▶ This is a very straightforward question. You should choose a principal (main) character from the novel. Before you explain why you would or would not like to be this character, you should think about the following questions:

- What exactly do I like or dislike about their life or their situation?
- How would I feel if I were in their situation?
- What do I think of their relationships with others?
- What kind of choices and opportunities do they have in life?
- What influence do they have over others?

Extract from Junior Certificate Marking Scheme, 2006:

Candidates may choose a character they would like to be, not like to be, or a character they have mixed feelings towards. Must give reasons for their choice.

Sample Answer

I have studied 'To Kill a Mockingbird', by Harper Lee. This novel is set in the fictional town of Maycomb, Alabama during the Great Depression of the 1930s. A character I would not like to be is Mayella Ewell, a young woman who falsely accuses a black man of rape. Mayella lives in filth and poverty and the novel's narrator, Scout Finch, describes her as 'the loneliest person in the world'.

One reason I would not like to be Mayella Ewell is that she lives in isolation. The whole town of Maycomb sees her family as 'trash'. They want nothing to do with her because she lives 'among pigs'. Scout's father says that the Ewells have been 'the disgrace of Maycomb for three generations' and no 'economic fluctuations' can change the way they live. In other words, there is no hope for the Ewells, as their circumstances will never change. Her father has never done a day's work in his life and he spends his 'relief checks' on whiskey. None of the Ewell children attend school or pass exams – the authorities have given up on them. Mayella is responsible for these children as her mother is dead and she has to take her place. When Atticus questions her in court, he asks her if she has any friends and she is shocked at this suggestion. This shows just how lonely and isolated she is. She also thinks he is making fun of her when he calls her 'ma'am' because no one has ever shown her respect before.

Mayella's living circumstances are filthy and degrading. The only beauty in her life is the geraniums which she keeps in old jars outside her house. Her home is a cabin which has been abandoned by 'negroes' on the edge of the town, right beside the black community and their cabins. This location shows that the Ewells are outside Maycomb society and their social status is as low as the status of black people in Maycomb (a very racist southern town). They also live beside a dump which suggests that they have been dumped by society, like 'trash'. The people of Maycomb want to forget about Mayella and her family, as they are an embarrassment to white people. The author tells us that every year 'Maycomb gave them Christmas baskets and the back of its hand'. This shows the hypocrisy of a Christian community that wants to seem charitable but also wants nothing to do with these people.

It is clear that there is no way out of Mayella's life, no hope. The above factors explain why she did the unthinkable and tried to 'tempt a negro'. When Mayella tried to seduce Tom Robinson, she had nothing to lose – no friends, no boyfriend, no self-respect, no respect in her community. It was an act of desperation and loneliness. She turned to Tom because he had been kind to her and she was desperate for affection. To add to the misery of her situation, it looks as if her father had sexually abused her before. Tom Robinson tells the court that when Mayella threw herself at him, she said she had never been with a man before and what her father did to her didn't count. It also becomes clear in court that her father must have beaten her up very badly when he found her with Tom Robinson.

By the time Mayella is finished in court, she emerges as a victim of poverty, ignorance, social isolation and a dysfunctional family. Even though the jury convicts Tom, no one truly believes her or her father. The trial is a humiliating experience for her and all her dark secrets become public. After the trial, her life will go on but it will not improve; if anything, her shame and isolation are made worse by the trial. Mayella also has to live with her conscience, knowing that she is ultimately responsible for Tom Robinson's death. For all of the above reasons, I would not like to be Mayella Ewell.

2005 Higher Level

Choose either the opening or the ending of a novel or short story you have studied.

(a) Briefly describe what happens in the opening or ending of your chosen text.

(10 marks)

(b) Did this opening or ending impress you? Explain your answer by reference to the novel or short story you have chosen.

(20 marks)

Approaching the Question

▶ It is important to have a detailed knowledge of the opening or ending of the novel before you attempt this question. Do not just summarise it! In planning this essay, you must think about what features or elements made the opening or ending impressive.

▶ You might refer to exposition, climax or denouement in your answer.

▶ The purpose of the opening is to set the scene, introduce the reader to the world and the characters and make the reader believe in the world of the story. The opening of a story is also called the 'exposition'.

▶ A story usually ends with climax and resolution (or denouement). The climax is the point in the story when tension is at its highest. The whole story builds up to this moment. The climax should be followed by a resolution, when all the issues or problems in the story are resolved or explained.

Extract from Junior Certificate Marking Scheme, 2005:

(a) 'Briefly describe' suggests a short, straightforward outline where the candidate simply describes what happens in either the beginning or ending of a novel or short story.

(b) Candidates may argue that the opening or ending did or did not impress them.

Sample Answer

(a)

I have studied 'To Kill a Mockingbird', by Harper Lee. This novel is set in a small American town in the 1930s and is narrated by Scout Finch, a young tomboy who lives with her father and older brother. The ending of this novel is powerful and dramatic as the two main characters, Scout and Jem, are almost killed are on their way home from a Hallowe'en pageant.

Scout and her brother, Jem, have to make a short journey home in the dark, but because of what happens it becomes the longest journey of their lives. Scout is dressed up as a ham in a costume made of chicken wire, so she can barely move. She describes it as a 'wire prison'. The children sense that they are being followed and they become frightened. They know they are in danger and they try to get home as fast as possible. Suddenly, they are attacked in the dark and Jem is knocked unconscious. Amidst the panic, someone who can't be seen grabs their attacker and saves their lives. This same person carries Jem towards the house.

When Scout gets home and the sheriff arrives, the mystery is quickly solved. They were followed and attacked by Bob Ewell, a violent, drunken man who had a grudge against their father, Atticus, who is a lawyer. Bob's daughter had accused a black man of rape, and Atticus had defended the man. Bob Ewell wanted revenge on Atticus, who had made him look foolish in court. The person who saved their lives was Boo Radley, their mysterious neighbour who hadn't left his house for years. The children had been obsessed with him when they were small and Scout still dreamed of seeing Boo Radley some day. In a strange and unexpected way, her dream came true because she finally got to meet Boo Radley.

(b)

The ending of this novel impressed me because of its powerful, exciting climax and its satisfying resolution. The climax was powerful because it was full of fear and suspense. The children are very vulnerable as they make their way home in the dark, with Scout almost trapped in her wire costume. The reader knows that Bob Ewell has been making threats beforehand, so there is a strong sense of danger. The description of their 'longest journey together' is excellent – they have the horrible sense that someone is following them and the presence behind them is close and persistent. It is too dark to see this presence, so Scout calls him 'shuffle feet' and 'our company'. They hope someone is playing a joke on them, but they quickly realise that this is no joke. These details impressed me because they made this scene compelling and realistic.

The panic and confusion is also well described. I was impressed by the way the author used Scout's costume to great effect. The image of Scout dressed up as a ham was very funny at first, but then it turned into a 'wire prison', and in an exciting twist it actually saved her life.

What impressed me most about the ending was the revelation of Boo, because it was a very rewarding ending to the novel. Most of Part One of the novel centred on the 'malevolent phantom', and the children's determination to make

Boo Radley come out of his house. As a reader, I was just as fascinated by the mystery of Boo Radley and longed to see him. He had played such an important role in the children's childhood that I felt as if the whole novel was building up to this moment. Scout no longer believed he was a 'malevolent phantom' but she still longed to see him before she died. Scout's wish was granted, and she also got to see that Boo was another 'mockingbird'. This was also an impressive ending, because good triumphed over evil. Boo did something very heroic, while Bob Ewell was finally punished for all he had done.

When Scout stood on Boo's porch, she finally saw things from his point of view. At that moment, she realised that Boo had been watching over them all along, like a guardian angel. Her childhood flashed before her eyes and everything began to make sense. This moment shows that Scout has truly learned from Atticus's advice and wisdom:

'Atticus was right. One time he said you never really know a man until you stand in his shoes and walk around in them. Just standing on the Radley porch was enough.'

I enjoyed the ending because the climax was exciting, the mystery of Boo was resolved, and Scout really developed as a character. In my view, these factors made the ending both memorable and impressive.

2005 Higher Level

From a novel or short story you have studied choose a character who experiences change.

(a) Describe this character at the beginning of the novel or short story.
(10 marks)

(b) How has this character changed by the end of the novel or short story? Support your answer by reference to the text.
(20 marks)

Approaching the Question

▶ Choose one character who has definitely experienced change by the end of the novel. You should focus mainly on inner change or personal growth, but some outer changes are also relevant. For example, Scout starts to wear dresses and Jem experiences physical changes as he enters adolescence.

▶ Either Scout or Jem would be the most obvious choice because they are constantly developing and growing up throughout the novel. Give lots of examples from the story to show how they have changed over time.

Extract from Junior Certificate Marking Scheme, 2005:

- Any character is allowable: does not have to be central to novel/short story.
- Physical description alone is not sufficient.
- Candidates may refer to age, gender, personality, occupation, qualities, relationships with others, etc.
- Interpret 'change' liberally, e.g. ageing, growth, maturity, broader view, more understanding, perspective, etc.
- Change may refer to the realisation by others of existing difference, e.g. people (some) realise the true nature of Boo Radley; their view of him changes.

Sample Answer

(a)

I have studied 'To Kill a Mockingbird', by Harper Lee. The novel is set in the southern state of Alabama, in the 1930s, in the fictional town of Maycomb. This is often described as a 'coming-of-age' novel, because its central character, Scout Finch, grows up and learns a lot in the course of the novel. Scout passes from innocence and naivety to insight and maturity beyond her years.

At the start of the novel Jean Louise Finch, nicknamed Scout, is a six-year-old tomboy who can't bear to be seen as a girl. She rejects all signs of femininity, wears overalls instead of dresses and loves to play with boys. She also loves to fight boys, and is well able to beat up boys who are older than her. The people she admires are male – Atticus (her father), Jem (her brother) and her wild summertime friend, Dill. As her mother died when she was two, there is very little feminine influence in her life. When Jem wants to insult her, he only has to remind her that she is just a girl. Her aggression gets her into a lot of trouble and her father urges her to tame her temper: 'Try fighting with your head for a change.'

At times, Scout is a lonely child. She has no mother, no sisters or female friends. The boys frequently exclude her because she is a girl. She often turns to an older lady, Miss Maudie, for female company. One very important female role model for Scout is Calpurnia, the family's black maid. However, Scout is too stubborn and badly behaved to appreciate Calpurnia at the start of the novel: 'Calpurnia was something else again . . . I had felt her tyrannical presence as long as I could remember.'

Because Scout is naive and innocent, she believes everything she hears in the neighbourhood, including gossip, rumours and superstitions. This leads her to believe that her neighbour, Boo Radley, is a 'malevolent phantom' who eats live squirrels and has the power to freeze azaleas overnight. In fact, thanks to the town gossip, Stephanie Crawford, Scout believes that Boo is responsible for all bad things that happen in Maycomb. She also believes that he tried to stab his own father. She is inheriting the prejudiced outlook of Maycomb's citizens.

Scout is very outspoken and tactless. When her new friend, Dill, tells her he has no father, Scout embarrasses him with her blunt questioning. She is too immature to see that this is a sensitive subject for Dill. On her first day at school, she tells the teacher and the whole class far too much about a young boy called Walter Cunningham. Later, when Walter comes to her house for dinner, she criticises him for pouring syrup all over his dinner. She cannot see that he is so poor he has never even tasted syrup before.

Most of Scout's flaws at the start of the novel are due to innocence and immaturity as she is only six years old.

(b)

By the end of the novel, Scout has been changed by many events and experiences.

The most noticeable change is that she has grown out of fighting with her fists. She is slowly starting to accept her femininity and enjoy some aspects of being 'a lady'. When her Aunt Alexandra hosts a 'missionary tea', Scout assists her and is impressed by 'this world of women'. She even wears a dress, but she still has her trousers on underneath, which shows that she has not fully lost her tomboy spirit. She no longer hates being a girl, but knows she is more comfortable in the company of men: 'I was more at home in my father's world.' It is as if she has reached a compromise with society.

Scout is wiser because she has grown in her understanding of humanity. She is a more tolerant person and she has finally learnt not to judge someone until she has 'walked in his shoes' for a while. For instance, she now knows that the hated Mrs Dubose was brave and determined. Her nastiness could be explained by her drug addiction. Mr Dolphus Raymond was not an 'evil man' after all. He was actually more compassionate than most white people in Maycomb. She learns to admire her father and respect his work. She shows compassion when she sees Mayella Ewell in court. Mayella is widely regarded as 'trash', but Scout can see that she was possibly 'the loneliest person in the world'. She comes to love and admire Calpurnia, who leads a 'modest double life'.

Her maturity and growth are most evident in her changed attitude towards Boo Radley. Even before Scout meets Boo, she has grown out of the childhood obsession with making him come out. Like Dill, she is starting to understand why Boo has rejected society. Her attitude towards Boo shows her maturity and common sense: 'So many things had happened to us, Boo Radley was the least of our fears.' When Scout finally sees him, she greets him with warmth and understanding. She has come a long way from the superstitious child who believed Stephanie Crawford's wild rumours. Standing on his porch, she even sees Maycomb from his point of view.

Scout learns not to judge people and to see the good in them, but she also sees the worst in human nature. She learns that ignorance, prejudice and racism can bring out the worst in people – the Old Sarum bunch almost lynched Tom Robinson the night before the trial. She sees how the all-white jury convicts Tom Robinson of rape without any evidence that the rape actually took place. Luckily, Scout manages to survive three turbulent years without catching 'Maycomb's usual disease', racism. She also rejects Maycomb's caste system which separates 'fine folks' from everyone else. She comes to the conclusion that all people are equal; they are just 'folks'.

Scout's changes are all positive – at the end of the novel, she is wise and mature beyond her years.

2008 Ordinary Level

FICTION
E
Name a NOVEL or SHORT STORY you have studied in which something strange or unexpected happens.
Describe the event which happens.
How were people's lives affected by this event?
Did the author succeed in convincing you that this strange or unexpected event could really have happened? Explain why/why not.
(20 marks)

Approaching the Question
- You must name the novel and the author.
- There are many strange and unexpected events in *To Kill a Mockingbird*, so you should choose one event which you know very well. Describe the event clearly and accurately.
- You can describe how people's lives were affected in a big or a small way. Perhaps the event did not affect people very much.
- The third part of the question is about the way the event was described. You can say that the event was realistic/unrealistic, well described, gripping, believable, likely/unlikely to happen, etc.

Sample Answer

I have studied an American novel called 'To Kill a Mockingbird', by Harper Lee. This is about two children, Scout and Jem, who live with their father in a racist southern town called Maycomb. Their father, Atticus, is a lawyer and he is defending a black man called Tom Robinson who is accused of raping a white girl.

A very strange event happens one day when Scout and Jem see a diseased 'mad' dog coming down their street. Jem and Scout tell their maid, Calpurnia, and she rings the telephone operator to tell her that there is a 'mad dog' coming.

As this is an emergency, Calpurnia sends for the sheriff and Atticus. When they arrive, the sheriff asks Atticus to shoot the dog, but Atticus doesn't want to as he hasn't shot a gun in thirty years. The children are terrified because they think their father can't shoot guns and is 'feeble'. They never expect their father to act like a hero. In fact, until this event, they were always embarrassed by their father because he never did anything exciting or interesting. When Atticus kills the dog with one shot, people's lives are affected because he saves everyone from danger. The children's lives are also affected in a good way, because they now see Atticus as a hero. Their relationship with their father is made stronger, because they respect him more than ever and are really proud of him.

The author convinced me that this event could really have happened because it was so well described. I could just imagine the dog twitching and wobbling his way down the road. The tension was really good when Scout described time slowing down to a 'crawl' because she was terrified that Atticus would fail. It was really tense when Atticus's glasses fell to the ground and smashed, so that Atticus had to aim with his bad eye. The author's realistic description and the tension really convinced me that this event could have happened.

2007 Ordinary Level

FICTION

E

Name a NOVEL or SHORT STORY you have studied in which there is an element of fantasy.

Describe the element of fantasy in the novel or short story.

Describe how the life of an individual or of a group of people is changed by the element of fantasy.

(20 marks)

Approaching the Question

▶ The 'element of fantasy' in *To Kill a Mockingbird* is based on Boo Radley. In Part One, Jem, Scout and Dill have a fantasy idea of Boo as an evil monster. The rest of the neighbourhood, e.g. Miss Stephanie Crawford, also has fantasies about Boo.

▶ You could describe how this fantasy affects the children, Boo and the rest of the community.

Extract from Junior Certificate Marking Scheme, 2007

- Name novel or short story = 2 marks.
- Description of element of fantasy = 9 marks.
- Description of how the life of an individual or of a group changed by the element of fantasy = 9 marks.

Sample Answer

I have studied an American novel called 'To Kill a Mockingbird', by Harper Lee. This is about two children, Scout and Jem, who live with their father in a racist southern town called Maycomb. Jem and Scout are very imaginative children, and they spend most of their summer holidays playing a game called 'Boo Radley' which is based on their childhood fantasy.

Boo Radley is a mysterious man who has not been seen by neighbours in over fifteen years. His family keep to themselves so nobody knows much about the family secrets. As a result, people imagine all sorts of fantasies about Boo. The adults in Maycomb believe he tried to kill his father. One lady, Miss Stephanie Crawford, insists that she has seen him spying on her when she sleeps. Children won't go near the Radley garden and they won't eat pecan nuts which fall from the Radley tree because they think Radley pecans will kill them. Everybody thinks Boo is an evil phantom who eats live squirrels and causes flowers to freeze over. This is all part of the fantasy about Boo Radley.

Jem, Scout and Dill, their friend, take the fantasy one step further by playing Boo Radley. They make up a drama about his life and they re-enact all the stories they have heard about him. They also try to make him come out of his house.

The fantasy changes Jem and Scout's lives because it brings them closer to Boo and he becomes their protector. It also changes Boo's life because he is entertained by the children's games and fantasies. From watching the children playing Boo Radley and trying to make him come out, Boo becomes really fond of the children and eventually saves their lives. If it weren't for their childhood fantasy and the way it brought them closer to Boo, Jem and Scout would have been murdered, so their lives were clearly changed forever.

OR

2007 Ordinary Level

FICTION

E

Name a NOVEL or SHORT STORY you have studied in which something extraordinarily good or bad happens to an individual or a group of people.

- Describe what happened.
- Explain what caused it to happen.
- Describe how the life of the individual or of the group was changed by what happened.

(20 marks)

Approaching the Question

▶   There are lots of possibilities for this question in *To Kill a Mockingbird*.

Extraordinarily good:

- Boo saves Jem and Scout's lives.

Extraordinarily bad:

- The jury convicts Tom Robinson.
- The prison guards shoot Tom Robinson seventeen times.

Extract from Junior Certificate Marking Scheme, 2007

- Name novel or short story = 1 mark.
- Identification of something extraordinarily good or bad that happened = 1 mark.
- Describe what happened = 6 marks.
- Explain what caused it to happen = 6 marks.
- Describe how the life of the individual or group was changed by what happened = 6 marks.

Sample Answer

I have studied an American novel called 'To Kill a Mockingbird', by Harper Lee. This is about two children, Scout and Jem, who live with their father in a racist southern town called Maycomb. In this novel, a black man called Tom Robinson is falsely accused of raping a white woman, Mayella Ewell. An extraordinarily bad thing happens when he goes to court and an all-white, racist jury finds him guilty.

Mayella had tried to seduce Tom but her father caught her and beat her up. She then claimed that Tom had raped her. Nobody really believed Mayella's story and there was no medical evidence that she had been raped. However, the jury finds Tom guilty without a scrap of proof or evidence. This is 'extraordinarily bad' because rape is a capital offence and Tom will face the death penalty for a crime he did not commit.

The jury convicts Tom because they live in a very racist, ignorant society. When it's a black man's word against a white man's, the white man always wins. The jury doesn't value Tom's life because it is just the life of a black man to them. It doesn't really matter to the white community if a black man dies.

This verdict has a terrible effect on Tom. He gives up hope even though Atticus tells him he can appeal the sentence. One day, while he is in the prison yard, he tries to escape. He runs towards the wall but the guards shoot him seventeen times. When Tom Robinson loses his life, his wife and children lose a husband and father. It is an 'extraordinarily bad' outcome for him and his family.

2006 Ordinary Level

FICTION
E

Name a NOVEL or SHORT STORY you have studied in which a character undergoes a change.
- Describe the character at the beginning of the novel or short story.
- Explain who or what caused the character to change.
- Describe the character at the end.
- Did you prefer the character before or after the change had taken place? Give reasons for your answer.

(20 marks)

Approaching the Question
▶ For this question, you could write about Jem or Scout, as they both change a lot over time. The sample answer deals with Scout.

Extract from Junior Certificate Marking Scheme, 2006

- Description of character at the beginning of novel or short story = 5 marks.
- Explanation for character's change = 5 marks.
- Description of character at the end = 5 marks.
- Reasons for preferring the character before or after change = 5 marks.

Sample Answer

The novel I have studied is 'To Kill a Mockingbird', by Harper Lee. The main character in this novel is Scout, a young girl who lives with her brother, Jem, and her father, Atticus, a lawyer. In the course of this novel, Scout changes a lot as she grows up and becomes more mature and wise.

At the start of the novel, Scout is a typical tomboy. She wears trousers at a time when no girl would dream of wearing trousers (the 1930s) and she plays with boys like her brother and Dill, her friend. She also fights like the boys and frequently beats up boys who annoy her at school. She loves to be 'one of the boys' and hates being called a girl. Sometimes she is very lonely, as the boys don't always let her play with them. Scout is very outspoken and is always putting her foot in her mouth, offending people when she doesn't mean to. This gets her into trouble on her first day in school.

Scout changes as she gets more mature. Her father tells her to fight with her head and not her fists, so she tries hard to do this. This becomes more difficult, as Atticus is defending a black man accused of raping a white girl, and Scout has to ignore people when they call her father a 'nigger-lover'. However, she learns to walk away from fights as she does not want to disappoint Atticus.

Scout also becomes less prejudiced because she learns to see things from the other person's point of view. Scout learns to do this because Atticus keeps pointing her in the right direction and giving her good advice.

At the end of the novel, Scout is still a tomboy, but she is ready to become a 'lady'. She has stopped fighting, and she works out problems by thinking about them and discussing them with Jem. She is a much kinder person because she can now walk in the other person's shoes and see things from their point of view. She is very wise for her years.

Scout was definitely a much better person after the change had taken place but I liked her more at the beginning because she was very funny. The childish Scout at the beginning was a rebel who spoke her mind all the time. The way she went around insulting people and getting into trouble made the book very entertaining. At the end of the novel, she is more mature but I think she is not as much fun.

2005 Ordinary Level

FICTION

E

Name a NOVEL or SHORT STORY you have studied in which the writer describes one of the following:
- **an interesting character**
- **the achievement of something that seemed impossible**
- **an adventure.**

Describe how the writer tells us about one of these events in the novel or short story you have chosen.

Approaching the Question
▶ Remember: you only have to answer on one of the above headings.
▶ Interesting characters include: Atticus, Jem, Scout, Calpurnia, Mr Dolphus Raymond, Miss Maudie, Boo Radley.
▶ For 'the achievement of something that seemed impossible', you could write about the time that Atticus shot the mad dog.
▶ For an 'adventure', you could describe the time the children sneak into Boo Radley's garden and Jem loses his pants.

Extract from Junior Certificate Marking Scheme, 2005
- Name of novel/short story = 2 marks.
- Select a heading = 2 marks.
- Description of selected event = 16 marks.

Sample Answer
The novel I have studied is 'To Kill a Mockingbird', by Harper Lee. I have chosen to describe how the writer tells us about an adventure in this novel.

The main characters in this novel are a sister and brother, Scout and Jem. They live in Maycomb, Alabama, and every summer they play with a friend called Dill. Every day during their holidays, they play a game called 'Boo Radley'. Boo is a mysterious man who never leaves his house and the children believe he is an evil phantom.

On the last night of the summer holidays, Dill, Scout and Jem decide to sneak into Boo's garden after dark to see if they can peep in the window and get a look at Boo. This is a real adventure for the children because no other children would dare to step inside the Radley place. The author shows how the children are terrified but their curiosity is stronger than their fear. Dill is really excited because it was always his idea to make Boo come out.

As the children approach the porch, they see a big shadow moving and they start to run away in terror. As they are escaping, they hear the roar of a shotgun and they start to panic. They have to climb under the fence to get out, but Jem's trousers get tangled in the fence. He has no choice but to wriggle out of his trousers and come out in his underwear. The sound of the gunshot brings all the neighbours out and they are shocked to see Jem in his underwear. The children were warned not to go near the Radley place so they have to pretend that they were playing strip poker!

Everyone knows that Mr Nathan Radley will shoot again if anyone comes back into his garden but Jem has to get his pants back without Atticus (his dad) finding out. When he goes back for them, it is worse than the first time because he actually risks being shot. He finds his trousers folded on the fence, and they have been sewn up where he tore them.

The author described this adventure really well, because she showed how it was really exciting and dangerous. Even when the children escaped, they were not out of danger. She also made it mysterious at the end, when Jem found his trousers. It was one of many great adventures in this novel.

12. Cloze Test Activities

For each activity, use words from the vocabulary list to fill in the blanks. You may find a dictionary useful for this activity.

Characters

- conservative
- imaginative
- humour
- offensive
- bigoted
- sympathetic
- sensitive
- courteous
- unconventional
- tolerant
- hypocritical
- defiant
- progressive
- frustrated
- sensational
- proud

Miss Stephanie Crawford loves to gossip and tell _____ stories about Boo Radley.

Scout often gets into trouble because she is _____ of authority.

Although Atticus is _____ of most people's flaws, he describes the Ewells as a 'disgrace'.

Atticus's way of raising his children could be described as _____.

Aunt Alexandra is very _____ of her family name and her outlook is generally very _____.

Dill's lying and story-telling show that he is very _____ and talented.

Scout gets quickly _____ by school because she is ahead of the class and feels she is wasting her time there.

Many of the religious people in the novel preach Christianity in public but in private they are very unchristian; this shows that they are _____.

When people judge others before knowing them, they can be described as _____.

Dill shows his _____ nature when he breaks down and cries in court during Mr Gilmer's interrogation of Tom Robinson.

Mayella Ewell thinks Atticus is mocking her because he speaks to her in a _____ manner.

Mr Dolphus scandalises the community because of his _____ lifestyle.

Miss Maudie is more _____ towards Boo than most of her neighbours.

Jem trashes Mrs Dubose's camellias because he finds her language so _____.

Miss Maudie and Atticus share a sense of _____.

Society

- *prosperity*
- *insular*
- *conscience*
- *deprived*
- *justice*
- *inherit*
- *segregation*
- *bigots*

Maycomb grows inward, it is a close-knit community and it ignores the rest of the world; this makes it a very _____ environment.

Poor children like Walter Cunningham are _____ of a decent education because they spend so much time working.

Even in times of economic _____ the Ewells would live in poverty and be regarded as 'trash'.

Prejudiced people are often referred to as _____.

Atticus was fully committed to _____ and was determined to live by his _____.

Atticus did not want his children to _____ the racist attitudes of Maycomb.

Due to _____ laws, black people and white people attended separate schools and churches.

13. Test Yourself — Quotations from the Novel

Who said the following words? At what point in the novel did they say them, and what were they referring to?

'People said he went out at night when the moon was high, and peeped in windows.'

'There goes the meanest man ever God blew breath into.'

'Ain't no snot-nosed slut of a school-teacher ever born c'n make me do nothin'! You ain't makin' me go nowhere, missus.'

'Someone inside the house was laughing.'

'You are too young to understand it . . . but sometimes the bible in the hand of one man is worse than a whiskey bottle in the hand of – oh, of your father.'

'Looks like all of Maycomb was out tonight, in one way or another.'

'Grandma says it's bad enough he lets you all run wild, but now he's turned out a nigger-lover we'll never be able to walk the streets of Maycomb again. He's ruinin' the family, that's what he's doin'.'

'Atticus was feeble: he was nearly fifty.'

'He walked quickly, but I thought he moved like an underwater swimmer; time had slowed to a nauseating crawl.'

'I guess he decided he wouldn't shoot till he had to, and he had to today.'

'I couldn't go to church and worship God if I didn't try to help that man.'

'She was the bravest person I ever knew.'

'I thought her voice strange: she was talking like the rest of them.'

'We decided that it would be best for you to have some feminine influence.'

'His maddening superiority was unbearable these days.'

'A mob's always made up of people, no matter what.'

'Did you, during all this running, run for a doctor?'

'Maycomb gave them Christmas baskets, welfare money, and the back of its hand.'

'I felt right sorry for her, she seemed to try more'n the rest of 'em.'

'Cry about the hell white people give coloured folks, without even stopping to think that they're people, too.'

'She is the victim of cruel poverty and ignorance, but I cannot pity her: she is white.'

'Miss Jean Louise, stand up. Your father's passin'.'

'In our courts, when it's a white man's word against a black man's, the white man always wins. They're ugly, but those are the facts of life.'

'I think there's just one kind of folks. Folks.'

'We can educate 'em till we're blue in the face, we can try till we drop to make Christians out of 'em, but there's no lady safe in her bed these nights.'

'Seventeen bullet holes in him.'

'We are a democracy and Germany is a dictatorship . . . Over here we don't believe in persecuting anybody. Persecution comes from people who are prejudiced.'

'Thus began our longest journey together.'

'Bob Ewell fell on his knife, I can prove it.'

'To my way of thinkin', Mr Finch, taking the one man who's done you and this town a great service an' draggin' him with his shy ways into the limelight – to me, that's a sin.'

14. *To Kill a Mockingbird* Quiz

---

1. Jem was older than Scout by _____ years.

    5   4   3   1

2. Simon Finch came from:

London	❐
Texas	❐
Alabama	❐
Cornwall	❐

3. Dill came from:

Meridian	❐
New York	❐
Chicago	❐
Maycomb	❐

4. On the first day of school, Miss Caroline is insulted and reduced to tears by:

Walter	❐
Burris	❐
Little Chuck Little	❐
Scout	❐

5. Mr Radley is said to be:

as hard as nails ☐
straight as a line ☐
ramrod strict ☐
ramrod straight ☐

6. Cousin Francis is Aunt Alexandra's:

son ☐
nephew ☐
grandson ☐
cousin ☐

7. One gift which Boo Radley did NOT leave in the tree is:

a watch ☐
a spelling certificate ☐
gum ☐
soap ☐

8. Zeebo was the son of:

Heck Tate ☐
Calpurnia ☐
Reverend Sykes ☐
Mrs Merriweather ☐

9. 'Foot-washers' is a local name for:

Methodists ☐
holy people ☐
Unitarians ☐
Baptists ☐

10. The children erect a snowman and dress it up as:

Nathan Radley ☐
Mr Underwood ☐
Link Deas ☐
Mr Avery ☐

11. The mad dog belongs to:

Tim Johnson   ❐

Harry Johnson   ❐

Tom Johnson   ❐

Tom Jones   ❐

12. Jem destroys Mrs Dubose's:

azaleas   ❐

geraniums   ❐

camellias   ❐

tulips   ❐

13. When the children visit First Purchase, Calpurnia has an argument with:

Lula May   ❐

Lula   ❐

Eula   ❐

Delilah   ❐

14. Atticus is threatened by a gang from:

Old Idaho   ❐

Sarum   ❐

Old Sarum   ❐

Harlem   ❐

15. Mr Dolphus Raymond drinks:

whiskey   ❐

Coca-Cola   ❐

whiskey and Coca-Cola   ❐

Bourbon   ❐

16. Mayella Ewell's lawyer is called:

Mr Underwood   ❐

Link Deas   ❐

Mr Avery   ❐

Mr Gilmer   ❐

17. Mayella Ewell's middle name is:

Poppy ☐
Mary ☐
Violet ☐
Ann ☐

18. Mr Underwood's first name is:

Brandon ☐
Braxton ☐
Brett ☐
Branston ☐

19. In which year does the trial take place?

1932 ☐
1935 ☐
1934 ☐
1936 ☐

20. The 'most devout lady in Maycomb' is:

Miss Maudie ☐
Miss Rachel ☐
Miss Caroline Fisher ☐
Mrs Merriweather ☐

Answers on p. 108.

15. Relevant Dates in American History

1861–65	American Civil War
1865	Thirteenth Amendment guarantees a permanent end to slavery in all of the United States
1917	USA enters World War I
1920–33	Prohibition Era in the USA: the manufacture and sale of alcohol was prohibited by law
1926	Birth of Harper Lee in Monroeville, Alabama
1929	USA is plunged into the Great Depression by the Wall Street Crash
1931	Scottsboro Trial in Alabama (nine African-American men falsely accused of raping two white women)
1941	USA joins allied forces in World War II
1955	Rosa Parks, a black woman, refuses to give up her seat in the 'whites only' section of a bus
1955	Montgomery bus boycott begins
1956	Supreme Court outlaws segregation on buses
1960	*To Kill a Mockingbird* is published
1963	Martin Luther King delivers his most famous speech at the March on Washington
1964	Civil Rights Act makes racial discrimination illegal
1964	Martin Luther King wins the Nobel Peace Prize
1965	African-Americans in the southern states are given the right to vote
1968	Assassination of Martin Luther King by a white racist

16. Glossary

Chapter One

state legislature	state government
collard	type of cabbage
shingles	wooden roof tiles
flivver	type of car
beadle	town official
scold	gossip

Chapter Two

seceded from the Union	Alabama, and ten other southern states, broke away from the Union of American states because they wanted to keep slavery legal in the South. This started the Civil War.
the crash	Wall Street Crash of 1929 (collapse of the stock market)
WPA job	work that the government makes the unemployed do to 'earn' their welfare money (WPA = Works Progress Administration)

Chapter Three

cooties	body lice
hain't	ghost (haunt)
relief cheques	welfare payment for the unemployed

Chapter Four

scuppernong	type of grape

Chapter Five

foot-washing Baptist	refers to extremist Baptists in the novel; a reference to Christ washing his disciples' feet to show humility

Chapter Six

bob-white	bird call

Chapter Seven

hoo-dooing	a curse on somebody; or voodoo

Chapter Eight

Rosetta Stone	an ancient stone, bearing inscriptions in three languages, discovered in Egypt in 1799. The inscriptions related to a decree passed in 196BC.
Appomattox	place in Virginia where General Lee of the Confederate Army (southerners) surrendered to Union forces in 1865, bringing the Civil War to an end
morphodite	a shape (the snowman is the shape of Mr Avery)

Chapter Nine

runnin' a still	making whiskey illegally
Stonewall Jackson	a famous Confederate (southern) general

Chapter Ten

alist	leaning sideways

Chapter Eleven

a CSA pistol	Confederate Army pistol from the Civil War
philippic	a word of Greek origin, meaning a bitter verbal attack on somebody

Chapter Twelve

Shadrach	one of three Israelites thrown into the furnace by King Nebuchadnezzar (from the Old Testament)
habiliments	clothes
bootleggers	people who sold alcohol illegally
the Quarters	where black people lived (like servants' quarters)

Chapter Thirteen

shinny	alcohol
Rice Christians	poor people in Asia who converted to Christianity in exchange for rice from the missionaries
born in the objective case	always criticising
reconstruction rule	the reorganised government of the South after the Civil War

Chapter Fourteen

pink cotton penitentiary	pink cotton prison (femininity being imposed on Scout)

Chapter Fifteen

Old Sarum	area of Maycomb where the Cunninghams and poor farmers lived
Ku Klux Klan	secret gang of white racists based in Southern states. They came out at night to terrorise black people and were known for lynchings. In most cases, law enforcers turned a blind eye to them. Often associated with burning crosses, robes and the hoods worn over their faces.
snipe hunt	sending someone to hunt snipe is a practical joke, like sending them on a wild goose chase

Chapter Sixteen

Jitney Jungle	popular supermarket chain
Braxton Bragg	very unpopular Civil War general, a Confederate
Mennonites	group of Christians who reject much of modern technology (often confused with the Amish)
Nehi Cola	brand of cola

Chapter Seventeen

ruttin'	vulgar slang for having sexual intercourse

Chapter Eighteen

cotton gin   a machine used in the processing of raw cotton

Chapter Nineteen

buck   male, often used in a derogatory sense

Chapter Twenty

an old Uncle   southern term for mild, 'harmless', elderly black servant
Thomas Jefferson   third president of the United States; wrote the Declaration of Independence
Rockefeller   famous American millionaire

Chapter Twenty-One

to lean   to take sides
psychical   relating to psychic and/or supernatural matters

Chapter Twenty-Two

missionary teas   tea parties organised by southern women to support the work of the Christian
                              missionaries

Chapter Twenty-Three

capital offence   a crime punishable by the death penalty
a hung jury   a jury that cannot agree on a verdict
Cajuns   people of French ancestry in Louisiana

Chapter Twenty-Four

missionary circle   fundraising group who support the missionaries abroad (organise missionary teas)
people up there   people living in the northern states of the USA where black people would have
                              had more rights and equality; seen as hypocrites by Mrs Merriweather
Mrs Roosevelt   President Roosevelt's wife; campaigned against segregation

Chapter Twenty-Five

English Channel   Mrs Stephanie Crawford is compared to the famous route,
   of gossip   because she is a renowned route for gossip

Chapter Twenty-Six

The Grit Paper   a newspaper for poor white farmers
Elmer Davis   an American newscaster in the 1930s

Chapter Twenty-Seven

National Recovery Act   President Roosevelt's programme which attempted to tackle the Depression
dog Victrolas   old-fashioned record players
Ad Astra per Aspera   Latin phrase meaning 'To the stars through difficulties'
WPA   Works Progress Administration; a government programme aimed at dealing with
                              unemployment

Chapter Twenty-Eight

divinity   a type of sweet
Dixie   the Confederate army's marching song during the Civil War

Chapters Twenty-Nine to Thirty-One

No glossary required for these chapters.

Answers to Quiz

(See p. 100)

1. 4
2. Cornwall
3. Meridian
4. Burris
5. Ramrod straight
6. Grandson
7. Spelling certificate
8. Calpurnia
9. Baptists
10. Mr Avery
11. Camellias
12 Harry Johnson
13. Lula
14. Old Sarum
15. Coca-Cola
16. Mr Gilmer
17. Violet
18. Braxton
19. 1935
20. Mrs Merriweather